also by america's test kitchen

The Side Dish Bible

How to Cocktail

The Perfect Pie

Vegetables Illustrated

The Ultimate Burger

Spiced

The New Essentials Cookbook

Cook's Illustrated Revolutionary Recipes

Dinner Illustrated

Tasting Italy: A Culinary Journey

The Complete Diabetes Cookbook

The Complete Slow Cooker

The Complete Make-Ahead Cookbook

The Complete Mediterranean Cookbook

The Complete Vegetarian Cookbook

The Complete Cooking for Two Cookbook

Cooking at Home with Bridget and Julia

Just Add Sauce

How to Roast Everything

How to Braise Everything

Nutritious Delicious

What Good Cooks Know

Cook's Science

The Science of Good Cooking

The Perfect Cake

The Perfect Cookie

Bread Illustrated

Master of the Grill

Kitchen Smarts

Kitchen Hacks

100 Recipes: The Absolute Best Ways to Make the True Essentials

The New Family Cookbook

The America's Test Kitchen Cooking School Cookbook

The Cook's Illustrated Meat Book

The Cook's Illustrated Baking Book

The Cook's Illustrated Cookbook

The America's Test Kitchen Family Baking Book

America's Test Kitchen Twentieth Anniversary TV Show Cookbook

The Best of America's Test Kitchen (2007–2020 Editions)

The Complete America's Test Kitchen TV Show Cookbook 2001–2019

Mediterranean Instant Pot®

Instant Pot® Ace Blender Cookbook

Cook It in Your Dutch Oven

Sous Vide for Everybody

Air Fryer Perfection

Multicooker Perfection

Food Processor Perfection

Pressure Cooker Perfection

Vegan for Everybody

Naturally Sweet

Foolproof Preserving

Paleo Perfected

The How Can It Be Gluten-Free Cookbook: Volume 2

The How Can It Be Gluten-Free Cookbook

The Best Mexican Recipes

Slow Cooker Revolution Volume 2: The Easy-Prep Edition

Slow Cooker Revolution

The America's Test Kitchen D.I.Y. Cookbook

THE COOK'S ILLUSTRATED ALL-TIME BEST SERIES

All-Time Best Brunch

All-Time Best Dinners for Two

All-Time Best Sunday Suppers

All-Time Best Holiday Entertaining

All-Time Best Appetizers

All-Time Best Soups

COOK'S COUNTRY TITLES

One-Pan Wonders

Cook It in Cast Iron

Cook's Country Eats Local

The Complete Cook's Country TV Show Cookbook

FOR A FULL LISTING OF ALL OUR BOOKS

CooksIllustrated.com

AmericasTestKitchen.com

praise for america's test kitchen titles

Selected as the Cookbook Award Winner of 2019 in the Health and Special Diet Category
INTERNATIONAL ASSOCIATION OF CULINARY PROFESSIONALS (IACP) ON *THE COMPLETE DIABETES COOKBOOK*

"Diabetics and all health-conscious home cooks will find great information on almost every page."
BOOKLIST (STARRED REVIEW) ON *THE COMPLETE DIABETES COOKBOOK*

"True to its name, this smart and endlessly enlightening cookbook is about as definitive as it's possible to get in the modern vegetarian realm."
MEN'S JOURNAL ON *THE COMPLETE VEGETARIAN COOKBOOK*

Selected as an Amazon Best Book of 2015 in the Cookbooks and Food Writing Category
AMAZON ON *THE COMPLETE VEGETARIAN COOKBOOK*

"This is a wonderful, useful guide to healthy eating."
PUBLISHERS WEEKLY ON *NUTRITIOUS DELICIOUS*

"The sum total of exhaustive experimentation . . . anyone interested in gluten-free cookery simply shouldn't be without it."
NIGELLA LAWSON ON *THE HOW CAN IT BE GLUTEN-FREE COOKBOOK*

"The go-to gift book for newlyweds, small families, or empty nesters."
ORLANDO SENTINEL ON *THE COMPLETE COOKING FOR TWO COOKBOOK*

"Some 2,500 photos walk readers through 600 painstakingly tested recipes, leaving little room for error."
ASSOCIATED PRESS ON *THE AMERICA'S TEST KITCHEN COOKING SCHOOL COOKBOOK*

"This impressive installment from America's Test Kitchen equips readers with dozens of repertoire-worthy recipes. . . . This is a must-have for beginner cooks and more experienced ones who wish to sharpen their skills."
PUBLISHERS WEEKLY (STARRED REVIEW) ON *THE NEW ESSENTIALS COOKBOOK*

"If you're a home cook who loves long introductions that tell you why a dish works followed by lots of step-by-step hand holding, then you'll love *Vegetables Illustrated*."
THE WALL STREET JOURNAL ON *VEGETABLES ILLUSTRATED*

"The 21st-century *Fannie Farmer Cookbook* or *The Joy of Cooking*. If you had to have one cookbook and that's all you could have, this one would do it."
CBS SAN FRANCISCO ON *THE NEW FAMILY COOKBOOK*

"Some books impress by the sheer audacity of their ambition. Backed up by the magazine's famed mission to test every recipe relentlessly until it is the best it can be, this nearly 900-page volume lands with an authoritative wallop."
CHICAGO TRIBUNE ON *THE COOK'S ILLUSTRATED COOKBOOK*

"The book offers an impressive education for curious cake makers, new and experienced alike. A summation of 25 years of cake making at ATK, there are cakes for every taste."
THE WALL STREET JOURNAL ON *THE PERFECT CAKE*

"A terrifically accessible and useful guide to grilling in all its forms that sets a new bar for its competitors on the bookshelf. . . . The book is packed with practical advice, simple tips, and approachable recipes."
THE HUFFINGTON POST ON *THE PERFECT COOKIE*

"Cooks with a powerful sweet tooth should scoop up this well-researched recipe book for healthier takes on classic sweet treats."
BOOKLIST ON *NATURALLY SWEET*

Selected as the Cookbook Award Winner of 2017 in the Baking Category
INTERNATIONAL ASSOCIATION OF CULINARY PROFESSIONALS (IACP) ON *BREAD ILLUSTRATED*

"A one-volume kitchen seminar, addressing in one smart chapter after another the sometimes surprising whys behind a cook's best practices. . . . You get the myth, the theory, the science, and the proof, all rigorously interrogated as only America's Test Kitchen can do."
NPR ON *THE SCIENCE OF GOOD COOKING*

bowls

VIBRANT RECIPES WITH ENDLESS POSSIBILITIES

AMERICA'S TEST KITCHEN

Library of Congress Cataloging-in-Publication Data has been applied for.

ISBN 978-1-945256-97-4

America's Test Kitchen

21 Drydock Avenue, Boston, MA 02210

Manufactured in the United States of America

10 9 8 7 6 5 4 3 2 1

Distributed by Penguin Random House Publisher Services

Tel: 800.733.3000

Pictured on front cover **Turkey Meatball and Barley Bowl (page 88)**

Pictured on back cover **Ramen Zoodle Bowl (page 181), Creamy Corn Bucatini Bowl (page 140), Mediterranean Eggplant Soup with Lamb (page 164), Moroccan Chicken Salad Bowl (page 35), Rainbow Bowl (page 53), Spicy Basil Noodle Bowl (page 122), Shakshuka Bowl (page 97), Green Goodness Salad Bowl (page 17), Skillet Burrito Bowl (page 61), Seared Tuna Poke Bowl (page 30)**

Editorial Director, Books **Adam Kowit**

Executive Food Editor **Dan Zuccarello**

Deputy Food Editor **Stephanie Pixley**

Executive Managing Editor **Debra Hudak**

Senior Editors **Leah Colins and Russell Selander**

Associate Editor **Camila Chaparro**

Test Cook **Samantha Block**

Assistant Editors **Kelly Cormier and Brenna Donovan**

Art Director, Books **Lindsey Timko Chandler**

Deputy Art Directors **Allison Boales and Courtney Lentz**

Associate Art Director **Katie Barranger**

Photography Director **Julie Bozzo Cote**

Photography Producer **Meredith Mulcahy**

Senior Staff Photographers **Steve Klise and Daniel J. van Ackere**

Staff Photographer **Kevin White**

Additional Photography **Keller + Keller**

Food Styling **Catrine Kelty, Steve Klise, Ashley Moore, Marie Piraino, Elle Simone Scott, and Kendra Smith**

Photoshoot Kitchen Team

Photo Team Manager **Timothy McQuinn**

Assistant Test Cooks **Sarah Ewald, Hannah Fenton, Jacqueline Gochenouer, and Eric Haessler**

Senior Manager, Publishing Operations **Taylor Argenzio**

Imaging Manager **Lauren Robbins**

Production and Imaging Specialists **Tricia Neumyer, Dennis Noble, Jessica Voas, and Amanda Yong**

Copy Editor **Deri Reed**

Proofreader **Christine Corcoran Cox**

Indexer **Elizabeth Parson**

Chief Creative Officer **Jack Bishop**

Executive Editorial Directors **Julia Collin Davison and Bridget Lancaster**

contents

welcome to america's test kitchen

This book has been tested, written, and edited by the folks at America's Test Kitchen. Located in Boston's Seaport District in the historic Innovation and Design Building, it features 15,000 square feet of kitchen space including multiple photography and video studios. It is the home of *Cook's Illustrated* magazine and *Cook's Country* magazine and is the workday destination for more than 60 test cooks, editors, and cookware specialists. Our mission is to test recipes over and over again until we understand how and why they work and until we arrive at the best version.

We start the process of testing a recipe with a complete lack of preconceptions, which means that we accept no claim, no technique, and no recipe at face value. We simply assemble as many variations as possible, test a half-dozen of the most promising, and taste the results blind. We then construct our own recipe and continue to test it, varying ingredients, techniques, and cooking times until we reach a consensus. As we like to say in the test kitchen, "We make the mistakes so you don't have to." The result, we hope, is the best version of a particular recipe, but we realize that only you can be the final judge of our success (or failure). We use the same rigorous approach when we test equipment and taste ingredients.

All of this would not be possible without a belief that good cooking, much like good music, is based on a foundation of objective technique. Some people like spicy foods and others don't, but there is a right way to sauté, there is a best way to cook a pot roast, and there are measurable scientific principles involved in producing perfectly beaten, stable egg whites. Our ultimate goal is to investigate the fundamental principles of cooking to give you the techniques, tools, and ingredients you need to become a better cook. It is as simple as that.

To see what goes on behind the scenes at America's Test Kitchen, check out our social media channels for kitchen snapshots, exclusive content, video tips, and much more. You can watch us work (in our actual test kitchen) by tuning in to *America's Test Kitchen* or *Cook's Country* on public television or on our websites. Download our award-winning podcast *Proof*, which goes beyond recipes to solve food mysteries (AmericasTestKitchen.com/proof), or listen to test kitchen experts on public radio (SplendidTable.org) to hear insights that illuminate the truth about real home cooking. Want to hone your cooking skills or finally learn how to bake—with an America's Test Kitchen test cook? Enroll in one of our online cooking classes. And you can engage the next generation of home cooks with kid-tested recipes from America's Test Kitchen Kids.

However you choose to visit us, we welcome you into our kitchen, where you can stand by our side as we test our way to the best recipes in America.

facebook.com/AmericasTestKitchen
twitter.com/TestKitchen
youtube.com/AmericasTestKitchen
instagram.com/TestKitchen
pinterest.com/TestKitchen

AmericasTestKitchen.com
CooksIllustrated.com
CooksCountry.com
OnlineCookingSchool.com
AmericasTestKitchen.com/kids

getting
started

introduction

Move aside plates; bowls are taking over. The bowl approach to cooking combines veggies, proteins, and a tasty sauce over a base like greens or rice for a cohesive meal that satisfies with every bite. You might have stopped into a popular fast-casual restaurant to buy a grain bowl or salad bowl and, like us, loved the near-limitless options for customization with healthy yet hearty ingredients. We had to find an unfussy way to make them—often—at home.

In the test kitchen, we appreciate bowls because they're everything we love about cooking—creative, fun, delicious, and beautiful. Bowls promise the perfect solution for busy home cooks: a relatively fast, make-ahead-friendly meal that's great for lunch or dinner, the freedom to improvise, and the ability to capitalize on leftovers.

The ideal bowl balances creativity with ease, yet recipes can quickly grow far too involved or require tons of preparation and excessive ingredients. We wanted to find a way to streamline prep work and design recipes that were flexible enough to be practical for weeknight cooking. Short ingredient lists were a must. Plentiful make-ahead options, swap suggestions, and even some reliance on store-bought components kept our recipes fun and filling but not intimidating, bringing us closer to bowl bliss.

As we built bowl after bowl, we learned a few secrets to ensure success every time, from including the right combination of components (check out Anatomy of a Bowl on page 7) to finishing off bowls with flair (turn to The Art of Arranging on pages 12–13). Along the way we took inspiration from global flavors and restaurant favorites in bowls like Weeknight Bibimbap (page 63), Buddha Bowls (page 73), and Harvest Bowls (page 20). Building customization into our recipes opened the door to the best-ever bowls, allowing us to simplify to save time or go wild and top our bowls with astounding arrays of colorful components. What's the real secret to the perfect bowl meal? Make your bowl your way.

---

5 TIPS FOR BETTER BOWLS

Bowls provide ample opportunity to make the most of available ingredients while trying out new flavor combinations, and with our easy tips you'll quickly find bowl success.

Raid your pantry (and fridge)
Using what you have on hand as a starting point is the key to mastering the bowl lifestyle.

Make ingredients ahead
Having bowl components already prepared makes improvising bowls incredibly easy. Prep a few bases and sauces or toppings at the start of the week, and you'll have instant meals with variety for your weeknight dinners.

Vary colors and textures
Adding a unique arrangement of colors and textures to your bowl makes it visually beautiful as well as delicious.

Try out a new diet or cuisine
Vegan, vegetarian, gluten-free—there's a bowl for everyone! Challenge your palate, explore recipes from bold and exciting cuisines, and try out something new.

Choose quality over quantity
Packing on tons of toppings is one way to go, but we think you're better off adding a few quality, fresh ingredients that will taste amazing.

how to bowl

The number of bowl recipes and combinations is endless. For inspiration, dive into the first four chapters, organized by base: Salads, Grains and Beans, Noodles, and Soups. Or improvise your own creation; the Bowl Basics chapter offers make-ahead recipes for every component, from base to topping.

FIND THE RIGHT FIT

Other than some of the soups, all of the complete bowl recipes in this book serve 2, which means you can serve both at once or eat one and save one, and there are quite a few soup bowls that serve 4 if you want to feed a larger crowd. If you'd like to make a bigger batch of bowls, it's easy to double recipes. Each bowl includes a calorie count to help you decide if a recipe is right for you.

CUSTOMIZE IT

With each complete bowl recipe, you'll see a box with Customize It suggestions. Sometimes, these boxes give quick tips on making recipes easier with ingredient swaps, like using a store-bought dressing instead of homemade. You'll also see options to kick your bowl up a notch with elevated toppings, giving you the flexibility to have fun and be creative with your bowls when time allows. Many of the recipes include options for making bowls friendly for vegetarian and vegan diets, but you can also use your judgment to change up components to suit your dietary needs. With so many variations and easy swaps, changing just one ingredient ensures that you'll never be bored by your bowl.

COOK YOUR PANTRY

Using what you have in your pantry (and avoiding a dreaded extra trip to the grocery store) is the secret to a quick meal. Browse through the recipes in this book to find one with ingredients you already have available, and then turn those lackluster ingredients into supersatisfying meals. With cucumber, bell pepper, and flank steak, you can make a Thai Steak Salad Bowl (page 29) in a snap. Or use that bag of frozen

peas, some white rice, and eggs to make a Green Fried Rice Bowl (page 64). If you have spinach, linguine, and a lemon, you're halfway to a Lemony Linguine Bowl (page 137). Below you'll find a few suggestions for easy recipes you can make using pantry staples as a starting point.

IF YOU HAVE...	MAKE...
Chickpeas	Pantry Chickpea Bowl (page 98)
Rotisserie Chicken	Buffalo Chicken Bowl (page 26)
Ramen Noodles	Summer Ramen Bowl (page 113)
Canned Black Beans	Black Bean Soup (page 168)
Canned Tuna	Mediterranean Tuna Salad Bowl (page 33)
Frozen Edamame	Creamy Miso-Ginger Noodle Bowl (page 125)
Frozen Corn	Skillet Burrito Bowl (page 61)
Cauliflower Rice	Buddha Bowl (page 73)
Cannellini Beans	Shakshuka Bowl (page 97)
Sriracha	Sriracha-Lime Tofu Salad Bowl (page 19)

SIMPLIFY WITH SWAPS

Swapping out ingredients can help simplify and streamline the time it takes to make your bowl. While you'll find many suggestions for simplifying bowls in the Customize It section of each recipe, don't be afraid to go off-script and try out your own recipe changes. Replace bases, proteins, or toppings with others you have available to simplify any of the recipes.

BECOME A BOWL MASTER

It's surprisingly easy to turn your pantry into the ultimate bowl kitchen with premade components you can quickly grab and add to any bowl. This can be as simple as making bases and proteins ahead so that you can quickly throw together lunch or dinner, or it can mean going the extra mile to make your own toppings, dressings, and sauces. In the test kitchen, we found ourselves returning to some of our favorite toppings over and over again because we loved the instant boost they gave to even the simplest bowl. And as a bonus, we could make many of our favorite additions once, store them, and reuse them. Make a batch of Sautéed Cherry Tomatoes (page 205) ahead and you could have a Spinach Pesto Noodle Bowl (page 139) for dinner one night and a Polenta Bowl with Broccoli Rabe and Fried Eggs (page 101) the next. Or make Chipotle-Yogurt Sauce (page 226) to keep in your fridge and pack a Quinoa Taco Salad Bowl (page 24) or a Steak Fajita Salad Bowl (page 51) for lunch during the week.

IMPROVISE WITH BOWL BASICS

The Bowl Basics chapter at the back of the book includes bases, proteins, vegetables, toppings, and sauces and dressings that will help you to build all of the completed bowl recipes in the book. You can also use a combination of bases and toppings from throughout the chapter to improvise your own bowl recipe from scratch.

DOUBLE IT UP

The recipes for bases and proteins in the Bowl Basics chapter will make enough for 2 bowls, and many of the vegetables, toppings, and sauces will make enough for 4 bowls. If you like to prep your meals ahead, the recipes can be easily doubled, stored, and reused in a variety of bowls.

TAKE YOUR BOWL TO THE NEXT LEVEL

Elevating a bowl from basic to impressive doesn't have to be a daunting process. Making elements ahead or adding a quick store-bought flourish can easily enhance the overall flavor of your bowl, and using the tips below will ensure that you're always prepared to kick your bowl up a notch.

Pickle fruits and vegetables

A pickled element adds complex acidity to a bowl, but pickles can be more varied than just cucumbers (although we love those, too!). Try quick-pickling carrots, grapes, or onions and jalapeños (see pages 216–217). Once you have pickled fruits or vegetables on hand, you can add them to any bowl for an immediate boost.

Buy one sauce, make one sauce

Keep your favorite store-bought sauce or dressing on hand to give any bowl a flavor boost. Then make a second sauce (see pages 219–227) to store in your fridge. For variety, pick two sauces with contrasting flavors and textures: creamy versus bright, or nutty versus herbal.

Make one crunchy topping that lasts

A crunchy element makes any bowl better. Storebought options are fine, but making your own ensures great flavor and quality ingredients. Bonus: Many of our crunchy toppings stay crisp and fresh for weeks, like our Savory Seed Brittle (page 211) or Crispy Shallots (page 212).

Make even the basic elements interesting

Plain proteins or vegetables are fine additions to bowls, but adding flavor to one element can instantly boost the flavor of the whole. Try simple upgrades like turning broccoli into Sautéed Broccoli with Garlic and Thyme (page 203) or turning edamame into Gingery Stir-Fried Edamame (page 198).

anatomy of a bowl

There are no hard and fast rules with bowls, but in the test kitchen following a few guidelines gave us consistently delicious results. We prefer a bowl with an equal ratio of base to toppings to ensure that the base doesn't get lost and the toppings aren't overpowering. We also found that the most flavorful, texturally interesting bowls had elements from each of the below categories.

BASE

By switching out your base, such as changing greens to grains, you can make a recipe feel like an entirely new bowl. Toss your base with half of the sauce for the bowl and top with the rest to ensure flavor in every bite. Greens, grains, rice, beans, noodles, and broth all make great bases, but some make great toppings as well, such as adding black beans to a rice bowl or sprinkling wild rice over a salad base, as in our Harvest Bowl (page 20).

PROTEIN

Changing how the protein is cut can influence the texture of the bowl, so try out large pieces, cubes, shredded pieces, or ground protein. Even without meat, a vegan bowl can get plenty of protein from tofu, tempeh, beans, or even edamame. Many protein options can be made in advance, such as Pan-Seared Flank Steak (page 195) or Pan-Seared Tofu (page 198).

VEGETABLE

Vegetables boost a bowl's overall flavor, nutrition, visual appearance, and textural contrast. Don't be afraid to combine raw and cooked vegetables in the same bowl. Try cutting your vegetables in a new way to change up the overall appearance, such as shredding, chopping, slicing half moons, cutting matchsticks, cutting on the bias, or even peeling ribbons. And although vegetables are most common in bowls, fruit can serve the same purpose.

SAUCE

Beyond adding moisture and flavor, a sauce or dressing can give a bowl its character, be that Ranch, Green Goddess, or Miso-Ginger. A sauce can be as simple as store-bought, or more complex, and can vary in consistency from a thin vinaigrette to a creamy sauce like Spicy Avocado–Sour Cream Sauce (page 226). Bright sauces can also add a pop of color as well as a punch of extra flavor, like our vibrant Sriracha-Lime Vinaigrette (page 220).

CRUNCH

Without a crunchy element any bowl can be satisfactory, but we've found that this component is what really sets a bowl apart and puts it over the top. Some of our favorite crunchy elements are as simple as raw radish slices or bean sprouts, but we also love flavor-packed additions like Quick Sweet and Spicy Pickled Red Onions (page 217) or Frico Crumble (page 214).

pantry staple shopping guide

A well-stocked pantry makes bowl improvisation quick and simple, and using some basic pantry items you can easily throw together a bowl in a snap. We recommend keeping these basics in your pantry for effortless bowl building any time.

BEANS

Beans can be an excellent bowl base or topping, making them a must-have pantry item for bowl improvisation. Chickpeas, black beans, and white beans are all useful to have on hand to add instant bulk to any bowl, and they're conveniently ready to use straight from a can.

BROTHS

Broth isn't just for soups; it can also add more flavor than water when cooking grains (see pages 189–192). We often use chicken broth in both our soups and our grains. Our favorite is **SWANSON CHICKEN BROTH**. If you're vegetarian, you can substitute vegetable broth for chicken broth. Our favorite is **ORRINGTON FARMS VEGAN CHICKEN FLAVORED BROTH BASE & SEASONING**, which comes in a convenient powder form that's inexpensive and easy to keep in your pantry.

CHEESES

Whether shredded or crumbled, a little cheese goes a long way in adding flavor and texture. We like a sprinkle of feta or a shaving of Parmesan over the top of a bowl to add just a little extra rich, cheesy flavor; our favorites are **REAL GREEK FETA FETA CHEESE** and **BOAR'S HEAD PARMIGIANO-REGGIANO**. Or, to pack more of a punch, blue cheese or goat cheese make excellent final additions; our favorites are **ROTH BUTTERMILK BLUE CRUMBLES** and **LAURA CHENEL'S PURE GOAT MILK CHEESE ORIGINAL LOG**.

DRESSINGS

Dressings aren't just for salads; they can also add big, bold flavor to other bowls. We often strongly prefer to make our own dressings because the flavor is unbeatable. See pages 219–227 for our best recipes. But that doesn't mean that store-bought options are off-limits. Sometimes, they're the perfect time-saver to simplify your bowl. Ranch, blue cheese, or balsamic dressing can all be a great addition to bowls, but the variety of store-bought dressings is limitless, and keeping your favorite on hand means you'll always be ready to improvise.

HERBS

Fresh herbs add an instant flavor boost to bowls, but herbs often come in large bunches, so it's important to pick herbs that you'll be able to reuse. We love parsley, cilantro, and basil to add flavor to just about any recipe, but you could also keep mint or Thai basil on hand for bowls when you want to add an extra layer of flavor.

EASY STORE-BOUGHT TOPPERS

While we love making our own toppings, we also know that sometimes store-bought is best to cut down on prep time. Many pantry staples that you wouldn't suspect make excellent bowl toppers. Try crumbling tortilla chips on top for salty crunch; our favorite brand is **ON THE BORDER CAFÉ STYLE TORTILLA CHIPS**. Store-bought salsa also adds quick and easy flavor (and you can always eat the leftovers with those tortilla chips!), and there's a wide variety available, from mango salsa to black bean salsa, that can change up a bowl's flavors with no hassle. We love adding different types of pickles to bowls for a little extra brininess, and although we often make our own quick pickles, there are plenty of store-bought pickled vegetables that you can try out. We even like to add *giardiniera* (our favorite is **PASTENE GIAR-DINIERA**) or sauerkraut (our favorite is **EDEN ORGANIC SAUERKRAUT**) for an easy flavor boost.

NEXT-LEVEL STORE-BOUGHT TOPPERS

With toppings the sky is the limit; popcorn, plantain chips, sweet potato chips, Parmesan crisps, nori, or crispy chickpeas can all add amazing sweet, salty, or savory flavors to the bowls in this book. Nuts and seeds also make excellent additions for crunch and a nutritional boost, or try adding chopped dried fruit to your bowl for a chewy textural contrast.

NOODLES

Noodles can be a base on their own or a great addition to soup bowls. A noodle doesn't neces-sarily have to be a traditional pasta; we use rice noodles, earthy soba noodles, and thick, chewy udon noodles to change up our bowls, and we love using spiralized vegetable noodles, too. Some noodles we prefer fresh, like Chinese noodles and udon noodles, but dried noodles like spaghetti, rice noodles, and even packaged ramen noodles are excellent pantry staples for building noodle bowls. For more information on cooking pasta and noodles and spiralizing vegetable noodles, see page 193.

RICE AND GRAINS

We use a variety of different types of rice as the starting point for our bowls, including white rice, brown rice, and even black rice. We recommend keeping your favorite type of rice in your pantry to quickly cook up when needed, and you can even make a big batch ahead. For more information on cooking rice see pages 189–190. Instead of traditional rice, get creative (and healthy) by using cauliflower rice, which you can make at home or purchase from the grocery store premade. Hearty, healthy grains make for a substantial bowl base, and we use grains like quinoa, bulgur, and farro as a starting point to build a bowl that can hold up to hefty toppings. Like rice, we recommend keeping your favorite grain on hand to cook when needed. For more information on cooking grains see pages 189–192.

SAUCES

A drizzle of good sauce can add flavor or heat to a bowl, but having the right ingredients on hand makes it easier to throw together a homemade sauce in a pinch. Lemon and lime (both the juice and the zest) add a burst of fresh flavor to any sauce. Keep mayon-naise (our favorite is **BLUE PLATE REAL MAYONNAISE**) or vegan mayonnaise (our favorite is **HAMPTON CREEK JUST MAYO, ORIGINAL**) on hand to use as a base for creamy sauces. To add a little extra heat, sriracha and gochujang can't be beat, and they'll last in your pantry for a while. Soy sauce adds meaty, umami flavor to sauces and is an absolute must in your pantry. To take your sauces to the next level, tahini, miso, and hoisin are the perfect additions. With these basics you'll be able to whip up sauces like a professional. For more information on making your own sauces see pages 219–227.

SPICES

There are a few basics we turn to over and over, but upgrading your spice cabinet can help you to elevate your bowl's flavors. Beyond the standard salt and pepper, we love using cumin, paprika, turmeric, and five-spice powder as easy flavor-boosting starters. Or, for more advanced bowl flavors, consider keeping saffron and Sichuan peppercorns on hand (our favorites are **MORTON & BASSETT SAFFRON THREADS** and **SAVORY SPICE SHOP PEPPERCORNS, SZECHWAN**).

VEGETARIAN-FRIENDLY PROTEINS

Plenty of bowls are naturally vegetarian or vegan but still packed with protein, so if you're looking to add extra protein without adding meat, consider keeping your kitchen stocked with tofu (soft, firm, or extra-firm), tempeh, edamame (frozen works fine), nuts, seeds, and canned beans. For more vegetarian protein recipes see page 198.

kitchen equipment

Having the proper food preparation tools minimizes the time you spend making your bowls, and using quality storage containers ensures that your leftovers will stay fresh. Don't worry, we've done all the work for you by testing out the best equipment. Here are the test kitchen's favorite pieces of equipment to stock in your bowl kitchen.

SALAD SPINNER

The **OXO GOOD GRIPS SALAD SPINNER** works easily—with just one hand—and effectively removes water from a variety of greens, with good clearance under the basket to collect runoff. Its lid is simple to pull apart (and click back together) for easy cleaning and drying, and it's dishwasher-safe.

VEGETABLE PEELER

Don't be fooled by the **KUHN RIKON ORIGINAL SWISS PEELER'S** featherweight design. This Y-shaped peeler's razor-sharp blade and ridged guide ensure a smooth peel with minimal surface drag, which allowed us to use it both to peel vegetables and to turn vegetables like carrots and zucchini into ribbons.

GRATER

For shredding cheese or vegetables for our bowls, we prefer a flat grater that won't get food stuck inside over a box grater. The easy-to-store, flat **RÖSLE COARSE GRATER** makes shredding a breeze, thanks to big, sharp holes; a large surface for better efficiency; and a solid, rigid frame that enables continuous grating (rather than short bursts).

MANDOLINE

The simple **SWISSMAR BÖRNER ORIGINAL V-SLICER PLUS MANDOLINE** makes cuts effortlessly with stunningly precise results, which makes cutting vegetables evenly a surprisingly simple task. Its hat-shaped guard protects well, and cleanup and storage are a breeze thanks to its compact vertical caddy.

SPIRALIZER

Simple, intuitive, inexpensive, and stable, the **PADERNO WORLD CUISINE TRI-BLADE PLASTIC SPIRAL VEGETABLE SLICER** easily spiralizes zucchini, beets, and potatoes into even, consistent noodles and ribbons.

BENTO-STYLE LUNCH BOXES

For a lunchtime bowl, you can't beat a bento box, with convenient compartments to store toppings. The **MONBENTO MB SQUARE—LITCHI** has two 4-ounce containers that can be used together or separately—which allowed us to keep things separate when needed. Both containers are more than 2 inches deep, so it's easy to stir in and eat from them without spilling.

GLASS FOOD STORAGE CONTAINERS

With a plastic lid that latches easily and securely and an airtight, leakproof seal that won't drip or let moisture in, the **OXO GOOD GRIPS 8 CUP SMART SEAL RECTANGLE CONTAINER** is our top choice for glass storage.

PLASTIC FOOD STORAGE CONTAINER SETS

The **RUBBERMAID BRILLIANCE FOOD STORAGE CONTAINER SET, 10-PIECE** has everything you need for lunches and meal prep. The set comes with two 1.3-cup containers with lids, two 3.2-cup containers with lids, and one 9.6-cup container with lid. Each container is made of lightweight Tritan plastic and stays as clear and stain-free as glass, and its audibly snug seal won't leak, even upside down. Its flat top makes for secure, compact stacking. If you need extras, the containers are also available individually.

storing & serving

Bowls make for the perfect on-the-go lunch or speedy dinner. With just a little planning, it's easy to have premade bowls at your fingertips every day. Use our tips and tricks to ensure that your bowl will still taste great no matter when you eat it.

MAKE-AHEAD MAGIC

In the Bowl Basics chapter you'll find a wealth of information on making individual components for your bowls ahead of time along with easy storing and reheating info so that you can always be prepared to build a bowl.

While recipes may vary, we've found that there are some general guidelines on how long the different components of your bowl will stay fresh and delicious when made ahead.

Grains	3 days
Noodles	2 days
Proteins	2 days
Vegetables	2 days (some will last up to a week)
Sauces	3+ days (some will last a week or more)
Toppings	5+ days (some will last as long as a few weeks!)

KEEP YOUR GREENS GREEN

To store salad greens, we've found that drying them is as important as washing them. After spinning salad greens in a salad spinner, we like to blot greens dry with paper towels because we have found that even the best salad spinners don't dry greens completely. If you don't plan on using the greens immediately, you can refrigerate them in the spinner bowl with the lid firmly in place for several days. Nobody wants to buy a big bunch of herbs and watch half of them wilt. To get the most life out of your herbs, gently rinse and dry them (a salad spinner works perfectly) and then loosely roll them in a few sheets of paper towel. Then seal the roll of herbs in a zipper-lock bag and place it in the crisper drawer of your refrigerator.

BOWLS ON THE GO

Packing a bowl for lunch is easy and convenient, but there are a few tricks to help preserve the quality of your bowl. Sauces and dressings will turn your toppings soggy, so store them separately if you're packing a lunch or on-the-go dinner. You can purchase special containers to pack dressings in lunch boxes, or you can repurpose something like a mini Mason jar as a dressing container. Crunchy toppings are best stored separately to help keep them crisp and fresh.

HOT 'N COLD

We often give suggestions as to whether or not you should warm your toppings before you assemble your bowl. If you're planning to reheat one component but not the whole bowl, keep that component separate from the rest until you're ready to assemble. For example, salads are typically cold, but sometimes we like the toppings to be warmed. Grain, bean, and noodle bowls can be hot, cold, or even room temperature.

the art of arranging

The beauty of a bowl doesn't just lie in the flavors—with so many vibrantly hued ingredients, bowls can look as appetizing as they taste. It's easy enough to toss all the ingredients together, but we wanted to re-create the gorgeous, photo-ready bowls that have made this trend so popular. Surprisingly, we found that a few simple arrangements could take a bowl from boring to beautiful in seconds.

MAKE PILES

Section off your bowl toppings into small piles to highlight their colors and textures. Clumping the components together shows off each different element in your bowl.

GARNISH WITH HERBS

Herb leaves can be chopped or torn and sprinkled on top to add an extra pop of color along with fresh flavor. Whole leaves also make for a beautiful presentation that shows off the natural beauty of the herbs.

SHAPE PERFECT RICE

Artfully arrange your rice into a perfect circle by pressing it into a measuring cup, then flipping it upside down into your bowl. You can present other components around, or on top of, the rice circle.

ADD TEXTURE

Nobody wants to look at a bowl of mush. Add toppings with a variety of textures to make your bowl more interesting. Sprinkle a crunchy element on top for quick contrast, and try out components of different shapes and sizes in the same bowl to add some extra visual appeal.

LINE THINGS UP

Arrange components in neat rows along your bowl to create a striped effect. Try this technique with fruits and vegetables that are circular or semicircles, or use straight or matchstick-style vegetables for a completely different effect.

ADD COLOR

Fresh fruit and vegetables like pomegranate, tomatoes, oranges, or avocado can add a whole rainbow of colors to your bowl, making it as visually pleasing as it is appetizing. Try out different colors of common vegetables, like golden beets or purple cauliflower.

DRIZZLE SAUCE

Use your sauce as a final flourish. Try a zigzag motion to make striking lines, drizzle in a circular pattern to make a sauce spiral, or drop the sauce in polka dots. The more colorful, the better, to add extra contrast to your finished bowl!

FAN OUT SLICES

Sliced fruits and vegetables like mango, apple, avocado, or pear look beautiful arranged in a fan-like shape. Hold one end of the slices together, and then fan the slices outward.

MAKE AN AVOCADO ROSE

Enhance your bowl presentation by turning avocado slices into a rose, as in our Buddha Bowl (page 73).

1. Thinly slice ½ avocado and shingle slices in overlapping line with smaller ends pointing in the same direction. Starting with the larger end, roll slices inward to create a small spiral.

2. Continue rolling inward, using fingers to flatten down ends, and shape slices into a rose shape.

3. Complete spiral, using fingers to gently flatten outside edges. Use your hands or a silicone spatula to transfer the rose to your bowl.

salad
bowls

Green Goodness Salad Bowl

Serves 2 | Calories per Serving: 480

Why This Recipe Works To qualify as a green goddess bowl, a salad requires just one thing: green goddess dressing, which gets its herbaceous flavor and appealing hue from a wallop of herbs. We took the concept further by creating a "goodness" bowl filled with an abundance of green foods, including a base of baby spinach, convenient frozen edamame, and chopped toasted pistachios. Broccoli sounded nice but the raw florets were dull and harsh. Our quick-cooking Sautéed Broccoli has some nice char, which boosts its flavor and shows off its hidden shade of vibrant green. And what would a goodness bowl be without buttery avocado? Though it's not green, we threw in shredded chicken for added protein. Since classic green goddess dressing is a bit heavy, we lighten ours up by replacing mayonnaise with a combination of buttermilk and yogurt. Three herbs (chives, parsley, and dried tarragon) give the dressing plenty of color, and an anchovy adds savory depth. Any cooked chicken would work well in this bowl; see page 194 for two recipes.

4 ounces (4 cups) baby spinach
½ cup Green Goddess Dressing (page 224), divided
2 cups shredded cooked chicken
¾ cup Sautéed Broccoli with Garlic and Thyme (page 203)

½ ripe avocado, sliced thin
¼ cup frozen shelled edamame beans, thawed and patted dry
2 tablespoons toasted and chopped pistachios

Toss spinach with half of dressing to coat, then season with salt and pepper to taste. Divide among individual serving bowls then top with chicken, broccoli, avocado, and edamame. Drizzle with remaining dressing and sprinkle with pistachios. Serve.

■ **CUSTOMIZE IT**

Instead of broccoli	Try Pan-Roasted Asparagus (page 202).
Instead of spinach	Use arugula or romaine.
Simplify the dressing	Store-bought green goddess dressing or another creamy store-bought dressing would work.
Make it vegan	Use the Creamless Creamy Green Goddess Dressing (page 225; omit the anchovy) and swap the chicken for Pan-Seared Tofu (page 198).

Sriracha-Lime Tofu Salad Bowl

Serves 2 | Calories per Serving: 280

Why This Recipe Works This light and easy bowl shatters tofu's bland reputation and proves that vegetarian bowls can pack big flavor. Napa cabbage, scallion, red bell pepper, bean sprouts, and shredded carrot give the salad a fresh, slaw-like base. Our Pan-Seared Tofu, which calls for pressing the tofu to drain before browning it in a hot nonstick skillet, ensures each piece turns out creamy and custard-like, with a slightly crispy exterior. A sprinkling of grassy cilantro and sweet, anise-like Thai basil provides herbaceous accents. But the salad is really all about the dressing: a spicy-sweet-sour combo of lime juice, honey, fish sauce, sriracha, fresh ginger, and olive oil. The vinaigrette and vegetable mixture can be refrigerated separately for up to 24 hours for an easy-to-assemble lunch bowl. Serve with extra lime wedges alongside a bottle of sriracha for an added kick before diving in.

½ head napa cabbage, cored and shredded (6 cups)

1 scallion, sliced thin

¼ cup Sriracha-Lime Vinaigrette (page 220), divided

1 cup Pan-Seared Tofu (page 198)

1 carrot, peeled and shredded

½ red bell pepper, stemmed, seeded, and sliced thin

1 ounce (½ cup) bean sprouts

¼ cup fresh cilantro leaves

¼ cup chopped fresh Thai basil

Lime wedges

Sriracha

Toss cabbage and scallion with half of vinaigrette to coat, then season with salt and pepper to taste. Divide among individual serving bowls then top with tofu, carrot, bell pepper, bean sprouts, cilantro, and basil. Drizzle with remaining vinaigrette. Serve with lime wedges and sriracha.

■ CUSTOMIZE IT

Make it meaty	Instead of tofu, Pan-Seared Flank Steak (page 195) or Sautéed Shrimp (page 197) would work well.
Instead of Thai basil	Fresh mint or basil both work as a substitute.

Harvest Bowl

Serves 2 | Calories per Serving: 400

Why This Recipe Works A nod to its autumnal ingredients, this harvest bowl is the perfect way to feature caramelized roasted root vegetables in a satisfying salad. We especially liked sweet potatoes for their light earthiness and sweet notes. To carry the harvest theme all the way through, we whisked up a cider and caraway vinaigrette, toasting and cracking the seeds but leaving them whole for appealing texture. For toppings, feta cheese added briny contrast and dried cranberries added color and more tartness. To crack caraway seeds, rock the bottom edge of a skillet over the toasted seeds on a cutting board until they crack.

4 teaspoons cider vinegar
1 tablespoon water
2 teaspoons Dijon mustard
1 teaspoon caraway seeds, toasted and cracked
⅛ teaspoon table salt
⅛ teaspoon pepper

2 tablespoons extra-virgin olive oil
4 ounces (4 cups) baby kale
1 cup Roasted Sweet Potatoes (page 209)
½ Granny Smith apple, cored and cut into ½-inch pieces
2 ounces feta cheese, crumbled (½ cup)
2 tablespoons dried cranberries

Whisk vinegar, water, mustard, caraway seeds, salt, and pepper together in bowl. While whisking constantly, slowly drizzle in oil until combined. Toss kale with half of vinaigrette to coat, then season with salt and pepper to taste. Divide among individual serving bowls then top with sweet potatoes and apple. Drizzle with remaining dressing and sprinkle with feta and dried cranberries. Serve.

■ CUSTOMIZE IT

Make it heartier	Wild rice may seem like an unusual salad topping, but the nutty, chewy grain would fit in perfectly here; see page 189. You could also add farro or wheat berries.
Add crunch	Our Savory Seed Brittle (page 211) would really kick this bowl up a notch. You could also use spiced nuts (page 210) or even plain toasted nuts.
Instead of kale	We love the convenience of prepackaged baby kale in this recipe, but feel free to substitute any mixture of dark tender greens.
Instead of sweet potatoes	Roasted Butternut Squash (page 203) would taste great here.

California Chicken Salad Bowl

Serves 2 | Calories per Serving: 430

Why This Recipe Works You can put avocado on just about anything and call it "California." We wanted to earn our West-Coast cred with a healthy and hearty salad that paid respect to the Golden State in every bite. Rather than just throw on diced avocado, we prepared a Creamy Avocado Dressing by pureeing ripe avocado with lemon, garlic, and olive oil for a luscious, dairy-free dressing. A California bowl should burst with fresh flavors, so we went heavy on the green veggies, while thinly sliced radishes offered a pop of color. To balance all the vegetal flavors, we added a handful of sweet grapes (think Napa Valley). Just when we thought we hit all the points, we realized we were missing something quintessentially Californian: a light, fluffy mound of alfalfa sprouts. We liked using Seared Chicken Breasts (page 194) here, but any cooked chicken would work.

- 4 ounces (4 cups) baby spinach
- 1 scallion, sliced thin
- ½ cup Creamy Avocado Dressing (page 224), divided
- 2 cups chopped cooked chicken
- 4 ounces seedless grapes, halved (¾ cup)
- 2 ounces sugar snap peas, strings removed, halved
- 4 radishes, trimmed, halved, and sliced thin
- 1 ounce (½ cup) alfalfa sprouts

Toss spinach and scallion with half of dressing to coat, then season with salt and pepper to taste. Divide among individual serving bowls, then top with chicken, grapes, snap peas, and radishes. Drizzle with remaining dressing and top with alfalfa sprouts. Serve.

■ CUSTOMIZE IT

Add crunch	Orange-Fennel Nuts (page 210) would add citrusy flavor, or a handful of plain roasted almonds would taste great.
Simplify the dressing	Use a light vinaigrette instead of avocado dressing and top the bowl with slices of avocado.
Instead of chicken	Chicken tastes great here, but you could also use Sautéed Shrimp (page 197) or Pan-Seared Tofu (page 198).
Make it heartier	Add some barley or quinoa for extra bulk.

Quinoa Taco Salad Bowl

Serves 2 | Calories per Serving: 360

Why This Recipe Works A taco salad bowl for the 21st century, this recipe ditches the deep-fried tortilla shell and replaces greasy meat with tender quinoa, which, with its hearty, chewy texture and nutty flavor, proved to be a remarkably good vegetarian stand-in for ground beef! Mixed with smoky chipotles in adobo, lime juice, and cilantro, the quinoa acquired a rich, spicy, even meaty taste. Instead of iceberg lettuce, we used slightly bitter escarole leaves as our base, which offered a bit more character and paired perfectly with rich and hearty but healthy toppings of avocado and black beans. Bright cherry tomatoes, sliced scallions, and an extra-hefty amount of cilantro completed the picture. Creamy, spicy Chipotle-Yogurt Sauce offered the perfect balance of heat from more chipotle chiles in adobo and cool from the yogurt.

1 cup cooked quinoa (page 189)
½ cup chopped fresh cilantro, divided
2 teaspoons lime juice
2 teaspoons extra-virgin olive oil
1 teaspoon minced canned chipotle chile in adobo sauce
½ small head escarole (6 ounces), trimmed and cut into 1-inch pieces

2 scallions, sliced thin
½ cup Chipotle-Yogurt Sauce (page 226), divided
½ cup canned black beans, rinsed
4 ounces cherry tomatoes, quartered
½ ripe avocado, sliced thin

Combine quinoa, ¼ cup cilantro, lime juice, oil, and chipotle in bowl and toss to coat; season with salt and pepper to taste. Toss escarole, scallions, and remaining ¼ cup cilantro with half of sauce to coat then season with salt and pepper to taste. Divide among individual serving bowls then top with quinoa mixture, beans, tomatoes, and avocado. Drizzle with remaining dressing. Serve.

■ **CUSTOMIZE IT**

Kick it up a notch	Crumbled queso fresco would add creamy texture here, or add feta cheese for briny, tangy flavor.
Instead of quinoa	You could use any hearty grain, such as farro, barley, or bulgur.
Instead of escarole	You could use any hearty salad green in this recipe.
Add crunch	Top with store-bought tortilla chips or homemade Crispy Tortilla Strips (page 215).

Buffalo Chicken Bowl

Serves 2 | Calories per Serving: 380

Why This Recipe Works Creamy, tangy, and with plenty of kick, this Buffalo bowl translates the appeal of the popular bar snack to a healthier salad suitable for enjoyment any day. Convenient coleslaw mix offered a sturdy base for our salad, but its meager quantity of carrot was barely noticeable, so we shredded an additional carrot. To bring together the iconic pairing of Buffalo sauce and blue cheese, we used our Blue Cheese Dressing, a lighter version of the classic using yogurt mixed with hot sauce, lemon juice, garlic, and pungent blue cheese. And it wouldn't be a Buffalo bowl without celery, sliced on the bias into attractive strips. Extra blue cheese on top added even more rich, tangy goodness. Any shredded cooked chicken would work in this bowl; see page 194 for two recipes. For the hot sauce, Frank's RedHot Original Cayenne Pepper Sauce is the classic choice for this dish.

¾ cup Blue Cheese Dressing (page 223)
1–1½ tablespoons hot sauce
4 cups (8 ounces) shredded coleslaw mix
2 cups shredded cooked chicken

1 carrot, peeled and shredded (½ cup)
1 celery rib, sliced thin on bias, plus ¼ cup celery leaves
2 tablespoons crumbled blue cheese

Whisk dressing and hot sauce together in bowl. Toss coleslaw mix with half of dressing to coat, then season with salt and pepper to taste. Toss chicken and carrot with remaining dressing to coat. Divide dressed coleslaw mix among individual serving bowls then top with dressed chicken mixture, celery, and blue cheese. Serve.

■ CUSTOMIZE IT

Simplify the dressing	Store-bought blue cheese dressing would be a little heavier than our homemade version, but it would work just as well.
Add crunch	Our homemade Croutons (page 215) taste rich and buttery, or you could use store-bought croutons.
Make it vegetarian	Substitute Roasted Cauliflower (page 205) for the chicken.
Instead of blue cheese	If blue cheese isn't your favorite, omit the crumbles. For the dressing, store-bought or homemade Ranch Dressing (page 223) would taste great.

Thai Steak Salad Bowl

Serves 2 | Calories per Serving: 390

Why This Recipe Works In the test kitchen, we love a good steak salad—volunteers flock to the tasting table whenever a new version appears. One of our favorite renditions, a Thai-style salad, combines char-grilled steak with fragrant herbs and a bright, bracing dressing. For a simpler but equally stunning take we opted to pan-sear flank steak. An easily whisked-together dressing—lime juice, fish sauce, shallot, oil, and pantry-friendly chili-garlic sauce—offered bold but balanced flavor. Bibb lettuce added a buttery texture while fresh cucumber and bell pepper delivered satisfying crunch. An abundance of fresh mint and cilantro were a must to round out the Thai flavors of our salad.

1 shallot, sliced thin
2 tablespoons vegetable oil
2 tablespoons lime juice, plus lime wedges for serving (2 limes)
1 tablespoon fish sauce
1 tablespoon water
1 teaspoon Asian chili-garlic sauce
½ head Bibb lettuce (4 ounces), torn into 1-inch pieces

1 recipe Pan-Seared Flank Steak (page 195)
½ English cucumber, halved lengthwise and sliced thin
½ red bell pepper, stemmed, seeded, and sliced thin
½ cup fresh mint leaves, torn
½ cup fresh cilantro leaves

Whisk shallot, oil, lime juice, fish sauce, water, and chili-garlic sauce together in bowl. Toss lettuce with half of vinaigrette to coat, then season with salt and pepper to taste. Divide among individual serving bowls then top with steak, cucumber, bell pepper, mint, and cilantro. Drizzle with remaining vinaigrette. Serve with lime wedges.

■ CUSTOMIZE IT

Kick it up a notch | Our Crispy Rice Noodles (page 215) quickly puff up into a dreamily light, crunchy topping that would pair well with the Asian-inspired flavors of this bowl. A handful of chopped peanuts would also work.

Instead of beef | Substitute Sautéed Shrimp (page 197) or Pan-Seared Tofu (page 198).

Seared Tuna Poke Bowl

Serves 2 | Calories per Serving: 430

Why This Recipe Works Sushi lovers, meet your new favorite lunch bowl. This delectable Hawaiian dish of superfresh tuna (traditionally served raw, but here seared to give it a crisp, browned exterior and deeper flavor) is brightly flavorful and endlessly customizable. Poke bowl restaurants often serve the bowls over rice, but we preferred a base of delicate baby greens enlivened with finely chopped sweet onion. When it came to our toppings, we loved the floral sweetness of fresh mango and the creaminess of ripe avocado. A soy-honey-ginger dressing balanced our bowl with sweet and savory flavor. Most cooked proteins need time to rest before slicing, but cutting the tuna immediately prevented carryover cooking and maintained our preferred rare to medium-rare doneness. For tuna steaks cooked to medium, increase the cooking time in step 1 to about 4 minutes per side.

2 (4- to 6-ounce) tuna steaks, 1 inch thick	2 teaspoons grated fresh ginger
¼ teaspoon table salt	1 teaspoon honey
¼ teaspoon pepper	5 ounces (5 cups) mesclun
2 tablespoons plus 1 teaspoon extra-virgin olive oil, divided	½ Vidalia or Walla Walla onion, chopped fine
1 tablespoon rice vinegar	½ mango, peeled and sliced thin
1 tablespoon soy sauce	½ ripe avocado, sliced thin

1. Pat tuna dry with paper towels and sprinkle with salt and pepper. Heat 1 teaspoon oil in 10-inch nonstick skillet over medium-high heat until just smoking. Add tuna and cook until translucent red at center when checked with tip of paring knife and registers 110 degrees (for rare), 1 to 2 minutes per side. Transfer to cutting board and immediately cut into 1-inch pieces; set aside until ready to serve.

2. Whisk vinegar, soy sauce, ginger, and honey together in bowl. While whisking constantly, slowly drizzle in remaining 2 tablespoons oil until combined. Toss mesclun and onion with half of vinaigrette to coat, then season with salt and pepper to taste. Divide among individual serving bowls then top with tuna, mango, and avocado. Drizzle with remaining vinai-grette. Serve.

◼ CUSTOMIZE IT

Kick it up a notch	Quick Pickled Carrot Ribbons (page 217) would add tangy bite here. A crumble of nori would also make a pleasant umami flavor addition.
Add crunch	Toasted sesame seeds would work well—use black, white, or both.
Instead of tuna	Oven-Roasted Salmon (page 197) would work well here.
Instead of mesclun	Substitute baby spinach.
Instead of mango	Orange segments would also work well here.

Mediterranean Tuna Salad Bowl

Serves 2 | Calories per Serving: 390

Why This Recipe Works For a tuna salad that is fresh and bright rather than creamy, we bypassed the mayo and instead opened a jar of oil-packed sun-dried tomatoes. Their concentrated sweetness made the perfect enhancement to plain canned tuna, but we also used some of the oil from the jar to prepare a lemony vinaigrette to imbue every bite of our salad with warm Mediterranean flavor. Meaty cannellini beans and briny olives over a bed of tender Bibb lettuce brought salty, savory balance to the tart dressing. And what is tuna salad without some crisp celery? For prominent celery flavor we doubled up and used both the celery ribs and the leaves.

1 shallot, sliced thin	1 (5-ounce) can solid white tuna in water, drained and flaked
1½ tablespoons lemon juice	
1 teaspoon Dijon mustard	½ head Bibb lettuce (4 ounces), torn into 1-inch pieces
1 small garlic clove, minced	
¼ teaspoon table salt	½ cup canned cannellini beans, rinsed
¼ teaspoon pepper	2 celery ribs, sliced thin on bias, plus ¼ cup celery leaves
2 tablespoons oil-packed sun-dried tomatoes, rinsed, patted dry, and minced, plus 3 tablespoons sun-dried tomato oil	¼ cup pitted kalamata olives, sliced thin

1. Whisk shallot, lemon juice, mustard, garlic, salt, and pepper together in large bowl. While whisking constantly, slowly drizzle in sun-dried tomato oil until combined; set aside for 5 minutes.

2. Toss sun-dried tomatoes and tuna with 1 tablespoon vinaigrette to coat. In separate bowl, toss lettuce with 1 tablespoon vinaigrette to coat, then season with salt and pepper to taste. Divide lettuce among individual serving bowls then top with tuna mixture, beans, sliced celery, and olives. Drizzle with remaining 2 tablespoons vinaigrette and sprinkle with celery leaves. Serve.

■ CUSTOMIZE IT

Add crunch	Sprinkle a handful of pomegranate seeds and toasted pine nuts over the bowls, or use chopped toasted walnuts.
Instead of cannellini beans	Chickpeas would make a good substitute.
Make it vegan	Omit the tuna and double the amount of beans.
Instead of Bibb lettuce	Use baby spinach or sweet romaine.

Moroccan Chicken Salad Bowl

Serves 2 | Calories per Serving: 550

Why This Recipe Works Cooked chicken on a bed of greens can become a tired number. To put a new spin on this classic combo, we drew inspiration from the flavors of Morocco: apricots, lemon, and warm spices. To give our dressing complex flavor, we reached for garam masala, a spice blend of coriander, cumin, ginger, cinnamon, and black pepper. We also added a little more coriander and honey for depth. Blooming the spices in the microwave deepened their flavors for an even bolder dressing. Chickpeas echoed the Moroccan theme and lent heartiness, while chopped dried apricots added fresh sweetness to balance the spices of the dressing. Tossing half the dressing with our greens and drizzling the remaining dressing on just before serving made the flavors pop. Seared Chicken Breasts (page 194) add a nice textural contrast, but you could use any cooked chicken here.

3 tablespoons plus 1 teaspoon extra-virgin olive oil, divided

½ teaspoon garam masala

¼ teaspoon ground coriander

2 tablespoons lemon juice

1 teaspoon honey

¼ teaspoon table salt

¼ teaspoon pepper

1 romaine lettuce heart (6 ounces), cut into 1-inch pieces

2 ounces (2 cups) watercress

1 tablespoon minced fresh parsley

1 small shallot, sliced thin

2 cups cooked chicken

½ cup canned chickpeas, rinsed

¼ cup dried apricots, chopped coarse

1. Microwave 1 teaspoon oil, garam masala, and coriander in medium bowl until fragrant, about 30 seconds. Whisk lemon juice, honey, salt, and pepper into spice mixture until combined. While whisking constantly, drizzle in remaining 3 tablespoons oil until combined.

2. Toss romaine, watercress, parsley, and shallot with half of vinaigrette to coat, then season with salt and pepper to taste. Divide among individual serving bowls, then top with chicken, chickpeas, and apricots. Drizzle with remaining vinaigrette. Serve.

■ CUSTOMIZE IT

Make it vegan	Substitute Pan-Seared Tofu (page 198) or Crispy Tempeh (page 198) for the chicken.
Instead of watercress	Arugula would work just fine in this bowl.
Instead of dried apricots	A handful of golden raisins or dried figs would make a pleasant substitute.

Steakhouse Salad Bowl

Serves 2 | Calories per Serving: 400

Why This Recipe Works This sumptuous bowl combines juicy steak, elegant pear, bright quick-pickled fennel, and a bold dressing in a salad with all the allure of a steakhouse dinner. For starters, we opted for steak tips, which are inexpensive but full of delicious marbling. Thinly sliced fresh pear gave our salad subtle sweetness, while quickly pickled fennel (steeped for a mere 30 minutes) brought acidity, crunch, and a mild anise-like flavor. For a dressing, we were drawn to a sweet-savory cider and sage vinaigrette made by reducing apple cider to concentrate its flavor. Lastly, a quick shaving of Parmesan cheese brought the perfect amount of saltiness for a mouthwatering, weeknight steak dinner in a bowl. Sirloin steak tips, also known as flap meat, can be sold as whole steaks, cubes, and strips. To ensure uniform pieces, we prefer to purchase whole steaks and cut them ourselves.

8 ounces sirloin steak tips, trimmed and cut into 3-inch pieces
¼ teaspoon table salt
¼ teaspoon pepper
1 teaspoon vegetable oil
5 ounces (5 cups) baby arugula

¼ cup Apple Cider–Sage Vinaigrette (page 219)
½ ripe but firm pear, cored and sliced thin
½ cup chopped Quick Pickled Fennel (page 216)
1 ounce Parmesan cheese, shaved

1. Pat steak dry with paper towels and sprinkle with salt and pepper. Heat oil in 10-inch nonstick skillet over medium-high heat until just smoking. Add steak and cook until well browned all over and meat registers 125 degrees (for medium-rare), 8 to 10 minutes. Transfer to cutting board, tent with aluminum foil, and let rest for 5 minutes. Slice steak ¼ inch thick against grain.

2. Toss arugula with half of vinaigrette to coat then season with salt and pepper to taste. Divide among individual serving bowls then top with steak, pear, and fennel. Drizzle with remaining vinaigrette and top with Parmesan cheese. Serve.

■ CUSTOMIZE IT

Add crunch	Crispy Shallots (page 212) add savory, rich flavor and texture.
Instead of pears	Apples would make a fine substitute.
Instead of pickled fennel	Store-bought jarred *giardiniera* would work, or simply omit.
Simplify the dressing	Use your favorite store-bought apple cider vinaigrette.

Mediterranean Chopped Salad Bowl

Serves 2 | Calories per Serving: 310

Why This Recipe Works   The appeal of a chopped salad is that all the ingredients are cut to a uniform size so that you get a variety of flavors and textures in every bite. Virtually any ingredients may be used, which makes chopped salads incredibly customizable. Yet most versions are uninspired, laden with deli meats and cheeses and drowned in dressing. In contrast, we steered our chopped bowl in a Mediterranean direction, starting with escarole, which has a mild bitterness that pairs well with bold flavors. Next, we added chopped cucumbers and quartered grape tomatoes, first salting them to remove excess moisture. To make our salad hearty, instead of deli meat we incorporated nutty chickpeas and kalamata olives. Finally, for tangy bite, we added briny feta.

½ cucumber, halved lengthwise, seeded, and cut into ½-inch pieces
 2 ounces grape tomatoes, quartered
½ teaspoon table salt, divided
 2 tablespoons extra-virgin olive oil
 4 teaspoons lemon juice
¼ teaspoon pepper

½ small head escarole (6 ounces), trimmed and cut into 1-inch pieces
¼ cup pitted kalamata olives, chopped
 2 tablespoons chopped fresh parsley
 1 cup canned chickpeas, rinsed
 1 ounce feta cheese, crumbled (¼ cup)

1. Toss cucumber and tomatoes with ¼ teaspoon salt and let drain in colander for 15 minutes.

2. Whisk oil, lemon juice, remaining ¼ teaspoon salt, and pepper together in bowl. Toss escarole, olives, and parsley with half of vinaigrette to coat, then season with salt and pepper to taste. Divide among individual serving bowls then top with drained cucumber-tomato mixture, chickpeas, and feta. Drizzle with remaining vinaigrette. Serve.

■ CUSTOMIZE IT

Add crunch	Chopped toasted walnuts provide pleasant texture.
Instead of escarole	Use romaine.
Instead of feta	Goat cheese would add creamy tang to this salad.
Make it vegan	You can omit the feta and the bowl will still taste great.

Smoked Salmon Niçoise Bowl

Serves 2 | Calories per Serving: 320

Why This Recipe Works A beautifully composed salad niçoise makes for a lovely meal in a bowl, especially when topped with a luxurious piece of seared salmon or tuna. But preparing all the components can be daunting, so we streamlined this classic. For a bit of luxury on a weeknight, rather than cook a fillet we opted for convenient smoked salmon, which provided salty, smoky richness without any prep work. Green beans and potatoes are typical for this dish; we cooked both in a single pot, starting the potatoes first so that both would finish at the same time. Hard-boiled eggs are also a common addition, and our Easy-Peel Hard-Cooked Eggs ensure each egg emerges smooth and pristine. To complement the smoked salmon, we swapped out the traditional vinaigrette for a dill and sour cream dressing, which paired well not only with the fish but also the potatoes and green beans. Use small red potatoes measuring 1 to 2 inches in diameter.

8 ounces small red potatoes, unpeeled and halved

¼ teaspoon table salt, plus salt for blanching vegetables

4 ounces green beans, trimmed

⅓ cup sour cream

1 tablespoon lemon juice

1 tablespoon chopped fresh dill
Pinch pepper

5 ounces (5 cups) mesclun

2 Easy-Peel Hard-Cooked Eggs (page 199), halved

4 ounces sliced smoked salmon

¼ cup pitted kalamata olives, halved

1. Combine 2 cups ice and 2 cups water in bowl; set aside. Bring 2 quarts water to boil in large saucepan. Add potatoes and 2 teaspoons salt; return to boil and cook for 10 minutes. Add green beans and continue to cook until both vegetables are tender, about 4 minutes longer. Using slotted spoon, transfer vegetables to ice bath and let sit until cool, about 5 minutes. Drain well.

2. Whisk sour cream, lemon juice, 1 tablespoon water, dill, salt, and pepper together in bowl. Toss mesclun with half of dressing to coat then season with salt and pepper to taste. Divide among individual serving bowls, then top with potatoes, green beans, eggs, salmon, and olives. Drizzle with remaining dressing. Serve.

■ **CUSTOMIZE IT**

Instead of red potatoes	For a change of color, try using purple potatoes.
Instead of smoked salmon	Canned tuna is a traditional choice for this salad. To dress this salad up, Oven-Roasted Salmon (page 197) would also be delicious. For a fish-free version, use cooked chicken.
Simplify the dressing	Use a lemon vinaigrette, or substitute parsley for the dill.

Shrimp and Grapefruit Salad Bowl

Serves 2 | Calories per Serving: 470

Why This Recipe Works For an elegant, summery salad bowl with light and refreshing flavors, we paired sautéed shrimp with a bright, citrusy grapefruit relish. Our relish, a combination of sweet-tart grapefruit and herby basil, added aromatic accents that tasters loved. For our salad base, we found a combination of subtly bitter endive and baby spinach paired nicely with the sweetness from the grapefruit and didn't overwhelm the delicate shrimp. We kept our vinaigrette mild with just a touch of vinegar to avoid an overly tart salad. For added bulk, we tossed black beans with the vinaigrette and gave them a quick stint in the microwave, which helped them absorb the tangy flavors of the dressing. Both the shrimp and relish can be made up to 2 days ahead for easy last-minute assembly.

1½ teaspoons white wine vinegar
1 teaspoon minced shallot
1 teaspoon Dijon mustard
⅛ teaspoon table salt
2 tablespoons extra-virgin olive oil
½ cup canned black beans, rinsed

1 head Belgian endive (4 ounces), halved, cored, and sliced crosswise 1 inch thick
3 cups (3 ounces) baby spinach
1 recipe Sautéed Shrimp (page 197)
½ cup Grapefruit-Basil Relish (page 227)

1. Whisk vinegar, shallot, mustard, and salt together until combined. While whisking constantly, slowly drizzle in oil until combined. Combine 1 tablespoon vinaigrette and beans in bowl and microwave until fragrant, about 30 seconds. Set beans aside to cool slightly, about 5 minutes.

2. Toss endive and spinach with 1 tablespoon vinaigrette to coat, then season with salt and pepper to taste. Divide among individual serving bowls, then top with shrimp, relish, and beans. Drizzle with remaining vinaigrette. Serve.

■ CUSTOMIZE IT

Add crunch	Sprinkle a handful of toasted chopped pecans over the salad.
Instead of Grapefruit-Basil Relish	Grapefruit segments would work as a simplified substitute.
Instead of endive	Arugula pairs well with the spinach as a base.
Instead of black beans	You could substitute any other variety of canned bean.

Fattoush Salad Bowl

Serves 2 | Calories per Serving: 320

Why This Recipe Works Croutons are arguably the best part of any salad, but in the Mediterranean dish known as fattoush, toasted pita is the star of the show: the delicious dressing clings to the bite-size pita pieces to make a flavor-packed, substantial addition to a bowl full of fresh produce, herbs, and bright, citrusy sumac. To prevent the pita from becoming soggy, we coated the pieces in a thin layer of olive oil before toasting them in the oven and then crumbling them. A base of escarole offered some serious personality and a subtle bitterness, and chickpeas made for a great vegetarian protein. Since chickpeas can be bland, we warmed them briefly in the microwave in a little olive oil, lemon, and sumac; the heat softened the chickpeas' skins so they could soak up more of the marinade. A simple Tahini Sauce enlivened our salad with nutty tahini flavor and tart lemon juice. Sumac boasts a unique souring effect with a touch of sweetness. Be sure to leave some extra on the table for sprinkling.

2 teaspoons extra-virgin olive oil	½ small head escarole (6 ounces), trimmed and cut into 1-inch pieces
½ teaspoon lemon juice	¼ cup chopped fresh mint
¼ teaspoon ground sumac, plus extra for serving	2 scallions, sliced thin
⅛ teaspoon table salt	½ cup Tahini Sauce (page 222), divided
Pinch pepper	4 ounces cherry tomatoes, halved
½ cup canned chickpeas, rinsed	½ English cucumber, sliced thin
	½ cup Pita Crumble (page 214)

1. Whisk oil, lemon juice, sumac, salt, and pepper together in bowl until combined. Stir in chickpeas, then microwave until just warmed through, about 30 seconds. Set aside to cool, about 5 minutes.

2. Toss escarole, mint, and scallions with half of tahini sauce to coat, then season with salt and pepper to taste. Divide among individual serving bowls, then top with tomatoes, cucumber, and cooled chickpeas. Drizzle with remaining sauce and sprinkle with pita crumble and sumac to taste. Serve.

▧ CUSTOMIZE IT

Instead of pita crumble	Crumbled store-bought pita chips would work here.
Instead of escarole	Romaine is a good substitute.
Instead of tahini sauce	A lemon vinaigrette would also taste great as a dressing.

Winter Salad Bowl

Serves 2 | Calories per Serving: 410

Why This Recipe Works   Nothing beats comfort food in the middle of winter, but after a while it starts to weigh you down. This bowl highlights the roasted, robust side of vegetable salads and is sure to leave you satisfied on even the coldest day. Butternut squash's sweet, creamy interior and fennel's anise-like, satisfying crunch made the perfect duo, and Italian turkey sausage provided a meaty boost and complementary sweetness. To keep the cooking straightforward, we roasted the vegetables and sausage together on a preheated sheet pan, removing the sausage first while the vegetables continued cooking until tender and caramelized. For a base, we liked the idea of earthy kale, but raw kale can be tough on your jaw. Fortunately, a quick soak in hot water softened its bite. Our sweet-tart Pomegranate-Honey Vinaigrette accented the flavor of the squash and sausage. It's important to use very hot water (110 to 115 degrees) when soaking the kale or the leaves will be tough.

12 ounces butternut squash, peeled, seeded, and cut into ¾-inch pieces (2½ cups)

 1 small fennel bulb, stalks discarded, bulb halved, cored, and cut into ¾-inch pieces

 2 teaspoons extra-virgin olive oil

⅛ teaspoon ground cardamom

⅛ teaspoon ground cinnamon

   Pinch table salt

   Pinch pepper

 8 ounces sweet Italian turkey sausage

 4 ounces curly kale, stemmed and sliced crosswise into ½-inch-wide strips (7 cups)

¼ cup Pomegranate-Honey Vinaigrette (page 219), divided

1. Adjust oven rack to lowest position, place aluminum foil–lined rimmed baking sheet on rack, and heat oven to 450 degrees. Toss squash, fennel, oil, cardamom, cinnamon, salt, and pepper together in bowl. Remove sheet from oven, place sausage on 1 side of sheet, and spread vegetables in single layer next to sausage. Roast until sausage is spotty brown and registers 160 degrees, 10 to 15 minutes. Transfer sausage to cutting board; set aside.

2. Stir vegetables on sheet and continue to roast until tender and spotty brown, 5 to 10 minutes. Once sausage has cooled slightly, slice ½ inch thick on bias.

3. While vegetables finish cooking, place kale in bowl, cover with hot tap water, and let sit for 10 minutes. Swish kale around to remove grit, then drain and spin dry in salad spinner. Pat leaves dry with paper towels if still wet.

4. Toss kale with half of vinaigrette to coat, then season with salt and pepper to taste. Divide among individual serving bowls, then top with roasted vegetable mixture and sausage. Drizzle with remaining dressing. Serve.

■ CUSTOMIZE IT

Kick it up a notch	Shaved Parmesan cheese would add salty, umami flavor.
Add crunch	Sprinkle toasted pine nuts over the top of the salad.
Instead of kale	You can substitute 4 cups of a power greens or baby kale salad mix (usually a combination of baby spinach, kale, and Swiss chard) and skip step 3.
Simplify the dressing	A balsamic dressing would work as a substitute for the pomegranate vinaigrette.
Make it vegan	Omit the turkey sausage.

Kale Cobb Salad Bowl

Serves 2 | Calories per Serving: 450

Why This Recipe Works   With an array of components including eggs, avocados, tomato, chicken, and smoky bacon, Cobb salad has all the makings of a colorful bowl satisfying enough for lunch or dinner. Romaine is the classic choice for Cobb, but we found that the subtle flavor and light texture fell flat when we piled so many toppings on. Instead we turned to sturdier kale, which we tenderized in a hot water soak. After crisping up some bacon, we sautéed chicken in the rendered fat for added flavor. Our homemade Blue Cheese Dressing is made lighter with yogurt and blue cheese, garlic, and lemon juice. A simple but classic hard-cooked egg completed our Cobb salad. It's important to use very hot water (110 to 115 degrees) when soaking the kale or the leaves will be tough.

2 slices bacon, chopped fine

8 ounces boneless, skinless chicken breasts, trimmed and cut into ½-inch pieces

⅛ teaspoon table salt

⅛ teaspoon pepper

4 ounces kale, stemmed and sliced crosswise into ½-inch-wide strips (7 cups)

6 tablespoons Blue Cheese Dressing (page 223)

4 ounces cherry tomatoes, quartered

½ avocado, cut into ½-inch pieces

1 Easy-Peel Hard-Cooked Egg, quartered (page 119)

1. Cook bacon in 10-inch nonstick skillet over medium heat until crispy, 5 to 7 minutes. Using slotted spoon, transfer bacon to paper towel–lined plate to cool. Pat chicken dry with paper towels and sprinkle with salt and pepper. Add chicken to bacon drippings in skillet and cook over medium-high heat, stirring occasionally, until cooked through, 4 to 6 minutes. Set aside off heat until ready to serve.

2. Meanwhile, place kale in bowl, cover with hot tap water, and let sit for 10 minutes. Swish kale around to remove grit, then drain and spin dry in salad spinner. Pat leaves dry with paper towels if still wet.

3. Thin dressing with water as needed, then toss kale with half of dressing to coat and season with salt and pepper to taste. Divide among individual serving bowls then top with chicken, tomatoes, avocado, and egg. Drizzle with remaining dressing and sprinkle with bacon. Serve.

■ CUSTOMIZE IT

Kick it up a notch	We love the tangy bite of Quick Sweet and Spicy Pickled Red Onions (page 217).
Instead of kale	Substitute 4 cups of a power green or baby kale salad mix and skip step 2.
Simplify the dressing	Store-bought blue cheese dressing would be a little heavier than our homemade version, but it would work just as well.

Steak Fajita Salad Bowl

Serves 2 | Calories per Serving: 420

Why This Recipe Works The best part about fajitas is mixing and matching toppings to create layers of spicy, smoky, fresh flavors that work together in one delicious bite. Here we take the fajita out of its traditional tortilla wrapper to allow each element to shine. For simplicity, we used a 10-inch nonstick skillet instead of grilling. We first seared chili-spiced flank steak, flipping every minute to ensure even cooking, before quickly charring the fajita staples of bell pepper and red onion, adding in fresh corn for sweet pops of crunch. A spicy Chipotle-Yogurt Sauce offered creaminess cut with smoky richness. As a nod to the tortillas of traditional fajitas, Crispy Tortilla Strips added a welcome final crunch.

8 ounces flank steak, trimmed

½ teaspoon chipotle chile powder, divided

½ teaspoon table salt, divided

¼ teaspoon pepper

1 tablespoon vegetable oil, divided

1 green bell pepper, stemmed, seeded, and sliced thin

½ small red onion, sliced thin

1 ear corn, kernels cut from cob

1 tablespoon water

1 romaine lettuce heart (6 ounces), cut into 1-inch pieces

½ cup Chipotle-Yogurt Sauce (page 226), divided

¼ cup Crispy Tortilla Strips (page 215)

1. Pat steak dry with paper towels and sprinkle with ¼ teaspoon chile powder, ¼ teaspoon salt, and pepper. Heat 1 teaspoon oil in 10-inch nonstick skillet over medium-high heat until just smoking. Add steak and cook, turning every minute, until well browned on both sides and meat registers 130 degrees (for medium), 10 to 14 minutes. Transfer to cutting board, tent with aluminum foil, and let rest for 5 minutes.

2. While steak rests, heat remaining 2 teaspoons oil in now-empty skillet over medium-high heat until shimmering. Add bell pepper, onion, corn, water, remaining ¼ teaspoon chile powder, and remaining ¼ teaspoon salt. Cook, scraping up any browned bits, until peppers and onions are softened and browned, about 8 minutes.

3. Slice steak ¼ inch thick against grain. Toss lettuce with half of sauce to coat then season with salt and pepper to taste. Divide among individual serving bowls then top with steak and cooked vegetables. Drizzle with remaining sauce and sprinkle with tortilla strips. Serve.

■ CUSTOMIZE IT

Kick it up a notch	Dollop on our One-Minute Tomato and Black Bean Salsa (page 227) or your favorite store-bought salsa.
Instead of fresh corn	You could substitute ½ cup frozen corn.
Instead of Crispy Tortilla Strips	Sprinkle on your favorite crushed tortilla chips or Fritos.

Rainbow Bowl

Serves 2 | Calories per Serving: 560

Why This Recipe Works Arranging a rainbow of fruits and vegetables on a bed of greens makes a stunning presentation—and a healthful, nutritious meal—but we wanted a bowl that tasted as good as it looked. Cherry tomatoes and a segmented orange offered bright acidity, which we balanced with buttery avocado and crisp radishes for their peppery snap and cheerful pink hue. To contrast with all the raw vegetables, we roasted purply-red beets to bring out their natural sweetness (this can be done several days in advance). A refreshing dressing of orange juice, honey, and ginger highlighted our salad, but we still wanted protein. Crumbled tempeh promised a vegetarian-friendly option, but we struggled to give it great flavor. Our solution? Boiling the tempeh in water and soy sauce seasoned it wonderfully, and a quick shallow-fry in oil transformed it into a crunchy umami bomb.

1 orange

5 ounces (5 cups) baby arugula

¼ cup Orange-Ginger Vinaigrette (page 219), divided

4 ounces cherry tomatoes, halved

½ ripe avocado, cut into ½-inch pieces

4 radishes, trimmed, halved, and sliced thin

1½ cups chopped Roasted Beets (page 202)

1 recipe Crispy Tempeh (page 198)

Cut away peel and pith from orange. Holding fruit over bowl, use paring knife to slice between membranes to release segments. Toss arugula with half of vinaigrette to coat, then season with salt and pepper to taste. Divide among individual serving bowls, then top with orange segments, tomatoes, avocado, radishes, and beets. Drizzle with remaining vinaigrette and sprinkle with tempeh. Serve.

■ CUSTOMIZE IT

Instead of red radishes	Thinly sliced watermelon radishes would add beautiful color. They're larger than red radishes, so you'll only need one medium-size radish.
Kick it up a notch	Add crumbled blue cheese for rich, salty flavor.
Simplify the beets	You can buy roasted beets at some grocery stores, or you can grate raw beet—just be careful: raw beets will bleed their bright color onto the rest of the salad (and your hands).
Instead of tempeh	Use cooked chicken (page 194) or Sautéed Shrimp (page 197).

Meze Salad Bowl

Serves 2 | Calories per Serving: 410

Why This Recipe Works Loaded with pleasantly charred vegetables and briny halloumi cheese, this salad packs the flavors of a Greek meze spread into a vegetarian bowl. Halloumi, typically grilled, turned deliciously charred in a nonstick skillet. Traditional meze vegetables inspired our choices of eggplant, radicchio, and red peppers (all browned); zucchini (left raw); and jarred artichokes. An herbaceous honey-thyme vinaigrette contrasted the salty cheese and bitter radicchio. To slice zucchini, use a vegetable peeler to shave the length of the squash, rotating the squash 90 degrees between each slice.

2 tablespoons extra-virgin olive oil, divided
8 ounces eggplant, cut into ½-inch pieces
½ head radicchio (5 ounces), cored and cut into 1-inch pieces
½ red bell pepper, stemmed, seeded, and cut into ½-inch pieces
½ zucchini (4 ounces), trimmed and sliced lengthwise into ribbons
3 ounces halloumi cheese, sliced into ½-inch-thick slabs

2 tablespoons honey
1 teaspoon minced fresh thyme
1 garlic clove, minced
½ teaspoon grated lemon zest plus 2 tablespoons juice
⅛ teaspoon table salt
⅛ teaspoon pepper
½ cup jarred whole artichoke hearts packed in water, halved, rinsed, and patted dry

1. Heat 2 teaspoons oil in 12-inch nonstick skillet over medium-high heat until shimmering. Add eggplant and cook, stirring frequently, until tender and browned, 8 to 10 minutes. Add radicchio and bell pepper and continue cooking until wilted and beginning to char, about 4 minutes. Transfer to bowl; stir in zucchini and set aside.

2. Heat 1 teaspoon oil in now-empty skillet over medium heat until shimmering. Add halloumi in single layer and cook until golden brown, 2 to 4 minutes per side. Transfer cheese to cutting board and cut into ½-inch pieces.

3. Whisk honey, thyme, garlic, lemon zest and juice, salt, and pepper together in bowl. While whisking constantly, slowly drizzle in remaining 1 tablespoon oil until combined. Toss vegetable mixture with half of vinaigrette to coat, then season with salt and pepper to taste. Divide among individual serving bowls, then top with halloumi and artichokes. Drizzle with remaining vinaigrette. Serve.

■ CUSTOMIZE IT

Add crunch	Crunchy, spice-roasted Crispy Chickpeas (page 212) would add delicious bursts of flavor.
Instead of halloumi	Crumbled feta would work well as a substitute.

Bistro Salad Bowl

Serves 2 | Calories per Serving: 410

Why This Recipe Works Traditional salad Lyonnaise—a mound of peppery frisée softened by a warm bacon vinaigrette and topped with crisp bacon and runny egg—makes for a substantial, satisfying meal. For a heftier base, we balanced the frisée with crunchy romaine. After cooking our bacon, we used the rendered bacon fat to make a warm vinaigrette that softened the greens and mellowed their bite. Rather than fussy poached eggs, we turned to fried eggs as a simplified alternative that maintained the classic runny yolk. Crispy, quick-broiled baguette toast slices were perfect for dunking into the fried egg's creamy yolk.

4 (¼-inch-thick) slices baguette (sliced on bias)
2 teaspoons extra-virgin olive oil
⅛ teaspoon table salt, divided
⅛ teaspoon pepper, divided
3 slices bacon, cut into 1-inch pieces
1 small shallot, minced
2 tablespoons red wine vinegar

1 tablespoon water
2 teaspoons Dijon mustard
½ head frisée (3 ounces), cut into 1-inch pieces
½ romaine lettuce heart (3 ounces), cut into 1-inch pieces
1 recipe Fried Eggs (page 199)

1. Adjust oven rack 6 inches from broiler element and heat broiler. Arrange bread in single layer on aluminum foil–lined rimmed baking sheet. Brush tops with oil and sprinkle with pinch salt and pinch pepper. Broil until bread is deep golden brown, 60 to 90 seconds. Set aside until ready to serve.

2. Cook bacon in 10-inch nonstick skillet over medium heat until crisp, 5 to 7 minutes. Using slotted spoon, transfer bacon to paper towel–lined plate. Pour off all but 2 tablespoons fat from skillet. (If necessary, add oil to equal 2 tablespoons.) Add shallot and cook until softened, about 2 minutes. Off heat, whisk in vinegar, water, mustard, remaining pinch salt, and remaining pinch pepper, scraping up any browned bits. Transfer dressing to bowl and wipe skillet clean with paper towels.

3. Toss frisée and romaine with half of dressing to coat then season with salt and pepper to taste. Divide among individual serving bowls then top with fried eggs, bacon, and bread. Drizzle with remaining dressing. Serve.

■ CUSTOMIZE IT

Kick it up a notch	Sautéed Mushrooms with Shallots and Thyme (page 207) would add earthy umami flavor on top of this salad.
Instead of frisée	You could substitute escarole or a mix of hearty greens.
Instead of baguette	Homemade Croutons (page 215) work, or use store-bought croutons.

grain
& bean
bowls

Buddha Bowl

Skillet Burrito Bowl

Serves 2 | Calories per Serving: 760

Why This Recipe Works   To turn a fast-casual burrito bowl into an at-home dinner with a little elegance, we dressed up the simple rice and bean base with a creamy, spicy avocado sauce and rich flank steak. Our Spicy Avocado–Sour Cream Sauce, full of ripe avocado, balances the heat from spicy jalapeño with creamy, cooling sour cream. The secret to a base with thick, creamy texture was to mix half of the sauce with our rice and beans, which we punched up with garlic and a dusting of cumin. Pan-seared flank steak proved to be the perfect protein—the inexpensive cut turned tender and flavorful in a skillet, and as a bonus it was easy to make ahead and reheat before building our bowl. For a final burst of flavor, we sprinkled on quickly charred corn, cooked in the same skillet as our base, which brought out the kernels' hidden sweetness. We like this bowl with either warm or room-temperature steak.

2 teaspoons extra-virgin olive oil, divided
¾ cup fresh or frozen corn
¼ teaspoon table salt, divided
⅛ teaspoon pepper
2 cups cooked white rice (page 189)
½ cup canned black beans, rinsed
2 garlic cloves, minced
½ teaspoon ground cumin
½ cup Spicy Avocado–Sour Cream Sauce (page 226)
1 recipe Pan-Seared Flank Steak (page 195)
½ cup thinly sliced red onion
¼ cup fresh cilantro leaves

1. Heat 1 teaspoon oil in 12-inch nonstick skillet over medium-high heat until shimmering. Add corn, ⅛ teaspoon salt, and pepper and cook, stirring occasionally, until kernels begin to brown and pop, 6 to 8 minutes; transfer to bowl, cover with aluminum foil to keep warm, and set aside until ready to serve.

2. Heat remaining 1 teaspoon oil in now-empty skillet over medium-high heat until shimmering. Add rice, beans, and remaining ⅛ teaspoon salt and cook until warmed through, about 5 minutes. Stir in garlic and cumin and cook until fragrant, about 30 seconds. Toss rice mixture with half of avocado sauce to coat then season with salt and pepper to taste. Divide among individual serving bowls then top with seared corn, steak, and onion. Drizzle with remaining avocado sauce and sprinkle with cilantro. Serve.

■ **CUSTOMIZE IT**

Simplify the sauce	Substitute sour cream for the Spicy Avocado–Sour Cream Sauce and add avocado.
Kick it up a notch	Use Quick Sweet and Spicy Pickled Red Onions (page 217) in place of red onion.
Make it vegetarian	Substitute Roasted Bell Peppers (page 207) for the steak.

Weeknight Bibimbap

Serves 2 | Calories per Serving: 580

Why This Recipe Works The combination of rice, vegetables, and egg in Korean bibimbap is a grouping made in bowl heaven, but we knew we needed to minimize the preparation time and maximize flavor to turn this dish into a weeknight-friendly bowl for two. Traditional bibimbap can have a lengthy list of ingredients; one of our favorite versions also requires a hot stone pot that gives the rice base a crisped, crunchy texture. To bring this bowl home (without the stone pot), we started by cutting the sautéed veggie list to just spinach, carrots, and mushrooms. While they stayed warm, we fried up our cooked rice in the same pan. We gave the rice a few minutes in the pan before serving, which allowed it to develop a golden brown crunchy bottom. To top our bowls, we fried two eggs, which gave each bowl a runny yolk that combined with our gochujang sauce into a spicy-rich sauce. Store-bought kimchi, with its bold fermented flavor, was the ideal final accompaniment.

4 teaspoons vegetable oil, divided
5 ounces (5 cups) baby spinach
1 carrot, peeled and shredded
1 scallion, minced
1 tablespoon soy sauce
1 garlic clove, minced
1 teaspoon sugar

2 cups cooked white rice (page 189)
1 recipe Fried Eggs (page 199)
¾ cup Sautéed Mushrooms with Sesame and Ginger (page 207), warmed
½ cup kimchi, chopped coarse
2 tablespoons Gochujang Sauce (page 221)

1. Heat 1 teaspoon oil in 12-inch nonstick skillet over medium-high heat until shimmering. Add spinach, carrot, scallion, soy sauce, garlic, and sugar and cook, stirring frequently, until spinach is wilted and carrots are warmed through, 1 to 2 minutes. Transfer vegetables to bowl, cover with aluminum foil to keep warm, and set aside until ready to serve.

2. Heat remaining 1 tablespoon oil in now-empty skillet over medium-high heat until shimmering. Add rice and firmly press into compact, even layer, cover, and cook, without stirring, until rice begins to crisp, about 2 minutes. Uncover, reduce heat to medium, and continue to cook until bottom of rice is golden brown, 4 to 6 minutes. Season with salt and pepper to taste. Divide among individual serving bowls then top with spinach mixture, fried eggs, mushrooms, and kimchi. Drizzle with gochujang sauce. Serve.

■ **CUSTOMIZE IT**

Make it vegan	Omit the eggs and use vegan kimchi.
Make it meaty	Substitute Pan-Seared Flank Steak (page 195) for the mushrooms.
For extra crunch	Add bean sprouts or thinly sliced cucumber.

Green Fried Rice Bowl

Serves 2 | Calories per Serving: 570

Why This Recipe Works For a healthier, vibrant spin on takeout fried rice, we combined bold herbs (made into a paste to cling to every grain of rice), bright green vegetables, deliciously crisped rice, and a fried egg with a decadently runny yolk. A food processor does a better job of creating the herb paste than we could do by hand, but in a pinch you can mince the toasted garlic, cilantro, basil, spinach, and serrano yourself. You can substitute regular basil for the Thai basil in this recipe.

2 garlic cloves (1 whole unpeeled, 1 minced)

¼ cup fresh cilantro leaves

¼ cup fresh Thai basil leaves

5 ounces (5 cups) baby spinach, divided

1 serrano chile, stemmed, seeded, and chopped coarse

½ teaspoon table salt, divided

2 tablespoons plus 2 teaspoons vegetable oil, divided

4 ounces green beans, trimmed and halved

1 teaspoon grated fresh ginger

2 cups cooked white rice (page 189)

½ cup frozen peas

1 recipe Fried Eggs (page 199)

Lime wedges

1. Toast unpeeled garlic clove in 12-inch nonstick skillet over medium heat, shaking skillet occasionally, until softened and spotty brown, about 8 minutes. When garlic is cool enough to handle, discard skin and chop coarsely. Process chopped garlic, cilantro, basil, 1 cup spinach, serrano, and ⅛ teaspoon salt in food processor until finely chopped, about 15 seconds, scraping down sides of bowl as needed; set aside.

2. Heat 2 teaspoons oil in now-empty skillet over medium-high heat until shimmering. Add green beans and ⅛ teaspoon salt and cook until green beans are spotty brown, 1 to 2 minutes. Add remaining 4 cups spinach and cook until wilted, 1 to 2 minutes. Add ginger and minced garlic and cook until fragrant, about 30 seconds. Transfer vegetables to bowl, cover with aluminum foil to keep warm, and set aside until ready to serve.

3. Heat remaining 2 tablespoons oil in again-empty skillet over medium-high heat until shimmering. Add cooked rice, herb mixture, peas, and remaining ¼ teaspoon salt, stirring to combine, then firmly press into compact, even layer. Cover and cook, without stirring, until rice begins to crisp, about 2 minutes. Uncover, reduce heat to medium, and continue to cook until bottom of rice is golden brown, 4 to 6 minutes. Season with salt and pepper to taste. Divide among individual serving bowls then top with green bean mixture and fried eggs. Serve with lime wedges.

■ **CUSTOMIZE IT**

Kick it up a notch	Add Sautéed Broccoli with Garlic and Thyme (page 203).
For a nutrition boost	Substitute cooked brown rice for white.
Make it vegan	Substitute Pan-Seared Tofu (page 198) for the egg.

Sichuan Stir-Fry Bowl

Serves 2 | Calories per Serving: 540

Why This Recipe Works This Chinese-style bowl flips the meat and vegetable equation. Instead of starting with meat, we started with Sichuan green beans, a classic Chinese side dish, which we bulked up with hearty brown rice, then added just a little ground pork for protein and flavor. Sichuan peppercorns provided spicy heat, but they also brought something else, awakening the senses with a playful lip- and tongue-numbing effect. For a peppercorn sauce that would cling to every bean, we added a little cornstarch to our mixture. We let the beans char in the skillet and develop a deep caramelized flavor. Sliced water chestnuts upped the crunch factor, and just 4 ounces of ground pork added meatiness. If you don't have a spice grinder, you can grind the Sichuan peppercorns with a mortar and pestle.

1 teaspoon Sichuan peppercorns

3 tablespoons water

2 tablespoons soy sauce

1 teaspoon sugar

1 teaspoon toasted sesame oil

½ teaspoon cornstarch

1 teaspoon vegetable oil

12 ounces green beans, trimmed and halved crosswise

4 ounces ground pork

3 garlic cloves, minced

¼–½ teaspoon red pepper flakes

1 (8-ounce) can sliced water chestnuts, drained

2 cups cooked brown rice (page 189), warmed

¼ cup fresh cilantro leaves

1. Process Sichuan peppercorns in spice grinder until coarsely ground, about 30 seconds. Whisk ground peppercorns, water, soy sauce, sugar, sesame oil, and cornstarch together in bowl; set aside. Heat vegetable oil in 12-inch nonstick skillet over medium-high heat until just smoking. Add green beans and cook, stirring frequently, until green beans are shriveled and blackened in spots, 6 to 8 minutes.

2. Add pork and cook, breaking up meat with wooden spoon until no pink remains, about 2 minutes. Stir in garlic and pepper flakes and cook until fragrant, about 30 seconds. Whisk sauce to recombine then add to skillet along with water chestnuts and cook, stirring constantly, until sauce is thickened, about 15 seconds.

3. Divide rice among individual serving bowls then top with green bean mixture and sprinkle with cilantro. Serve.

■ **CUSTOMIZE IT**

Kick it up a notch	Add mandarin oranges for a burst of citrus.
For extra crunch	Sprinkle on chopped roasted cashews.

Tofu Sushi Bowl

Serves 2 | Calories per Serving: 530

Why This Recipe Works Sushi rolls can be both time-consuming and tedious to make, which is why they are often considered takeout fare. We wanted to develop a deconstructed version in a bowl that was easy to assemble at home with flavors inspired by sushi rolls. For simplicity, we kept it vegetarian with tofu, coating long fingers with cornstarch to help them brown to crispy perfection. Brown rice isn't typical for sushi rolls, but we liked the added nutritional value and nutty chew in our bowl base. Sushi rice is often seasoned, so we tossed our rice with Sesame-Scallion Vinaigrette to stand in for the classic sushi rice seasoning. For toppings we achieved a fresh, satisfying crunch from some thinly sliced radishes and cucumber. Sushi can't say no to avocado, and we loved its added richness. Some crumbled nori (to mimic the roll), scattered across the top of our sushi bowl sealed the deal. We like this bowl with either warm or room-temperature rice.

7 ounces firm tofu, cut into 3-inch-long by ½-inch-thick fingers

⅛ teaspoon table salt

⅛ teaspoon pepper

3 tablespoons cornstarch

1 tablespoon vegetable oil

2 cups cooked brown rice (page 189)

¼ cup Sesame-Scallion Vinaigrette (page 220)

3 radishes, sliced thin

½ cucumber, halved lengthwise, seeded, and sliced thin

½ ripe avocado, cubed

1 (8 by 7½-inch) sheet nori, crumbled

1. Spread tofu over paper towel–lined plate, let drain for 20 minutes, then gently pat dry with paper towels. Sprinkle with salt and pepper.

2. Gently toss drained tofu with cornstarch in bowl. Heat oil in 12-inch nonstick skillet over medium-high heat until shimmering. Add tofu and brown lightly on all sides, 12 to 15 minutes; transfer to clean paper towel–lined plate to drain.

3. Toss rice with half of vinaigrette to coat then season with salt and pepper to taste. Divide among individual serving bowls then top with tofu, radishes, cucumber, and avocado. Drizzle with remaining vinaigrette and sprinkle with nori. Serve.

■ CUSTOMIZE IT

Kick it up a notch	Add pickled ginger.
Simplify the dressing	Use a store-bought sesame vinaigrette instead of homemade.

Forbidden Rice Bowl with Salmon

Why This Recipe Works Black rice, also known as "forbidden rice," was once reserved for the emperors of China, so we turned this ancient grain into a bowl fit for royalty with a citrusy mirin-ginger dressing, deliciously rich salmon, and bright toppings. Black rice has a dark color and contains more protein, fiber, and iron than other rice varieties. To ensure well-seasoned grains with a bit of chew, we simply boiled the rice like pasta, and then seasoned it with a quick dressing full of bright lime juice, sweet mirin, and pungent ginger. For a protein boost, we roasted salmon fillets until medium-rare and then arranged them atop the rice. Skin-on salmon fillets hold together best during cooking, and the skin helps keep the fish moist. We kept the toppings light to contrast the dark rice with crisp cucumber and fresh cilantro. A final topping of radishes, sautéed to soften their harsh exterior and bring out their often hidden sweetness, added an earthy element. If you can't find black rice, use brown rice (page 189). For more information on shaping rice, see page 12.

2 tablespoons lime juice
2 tablespoons mirin
1 teaspoon grated fresh ginger
2 cups cooked black rice (page 189)
1 recipe Oven-Roasted Salmon (page 197)

1 cup Sautéed Radishes (page 208)
½ cucumber, halved lengthwise, seeded, and sliced thin
¼ cup fresh cilantro leaves

Whisk lime juice, mirin, and ginger together in small bowl. Toss rice with 1 tablespoon lime dressing to coat then season with salt and pepper to taste. Divide rice among individual serving bowls then top with salmon, radishes, and cucumber. Drizzle with remaining dressing then sprinkle with cilantro. Serve.

■ CUSTOMIZE IT

Kick it up a notch	Sprinkle 1 crumbled nori sheet over the top.
Instead of salmon	Use Sautéed Shrimp (page 197).
Instead of radishes	Use Pan-Roasted Asparagus (page 202).

Buddha Bowl

Serves 2 | Calories per Serving: 550

Why This Recipe Works   What is a Buddha bowl? The question may be unanswerable, we discovered, as our searches turned up hundreds of examples. So we chose our own path: a nourishing, vegan bowl that emphasizes vegetables as much as possible. In place of a grain we chose nutrient-rich cauliflower rice as our base, cooking it with red pepper flakes and turmeric to impart both spice and bright color. Roasted sweet potatoes, spinach, and ripe avocado added the perfect balance of nutrition, flavor, and texture. For a sauce, our creamless "creamy" roasted red pepper and tahini dressing, made with soaked cashews, tricks your taste buds with its dairy-free creamy texture and roasted, smoky flavor. Finally, a generous handful of crispy spiced chickpeas added crunchy bursts of flavor. While we prefer to make our own, you can substitute store-bought refrigerated or frozen cauliflower rice in a pinch; just be sure to reduce the covered cooking time in step 1 to about 10 minutes. For information on making the avocado into a rose, see page 13.

½ head cauliflower (1 pound), cored and cut into 1-inch florets (3 cups)
1 teaspoon extra-virgin olive oil
1 garlic clove, minced
⅛–¼ teaspoon red pepper flakes
¼ teaspoon ground turmeric
½ cup water
⅛ teaspoon table salt

1 cup baby spinach
1 cup Roasted Sweet Potatoes (page 209), warmed
1 ripe avocado, sliced thin
¼ cup Creamless Creamy Roasted Red Pepper and Tahini Dressing (page 225)
½ cup Indian-Spiced Crispy Chickpeas (page 212)

1. Pulse cauliflower in food processor until finely ground into ¼- to ⅛-inch pieces, 6 to 8 pulses, scraping down sides of bowl as needed. Heat oil in large saucepan over medium-low heat until shimmering. Add garlic, pepper flakes, and turmeric and cook until fragrant, about 30 seconds. Stir in processed cauliflower, water, and salt, cover, and cook, stirring occasionally, until cauliflower is tender, 12 to 15 minutes.

2. Uncover and continue to cook, stirring occasionally, until cauliflower rice is nearly dry, about 3 minutes. Stir in spinach and cook until spinach just begins to wilt, about 30 seconds. Season with salt and pepper to taste.

3. Divide cauliflower rice among individual serving bowls then top with sweet potatoes and avocado. Drizzle with tahini dressing and sprinkle with chickpeas. Serve.

■ CUSTOMIZE IT

Simplify the bowl	Use store-bought crispy chickpeas and your favorite bright-tasting, store-bought creamy dressing instead of homemade.
Kick it up a notch	Top with store-bought sauerkraut.

Italian Harvest Bowl

Serves 2 | Calories per Serving: 720

Why This Recipe Works Is there anything else like Italy in the fall? Not many of us have the luxury of strolling through the food markets of Tuscany in late September, but that doesn't mean we can't bring those flavors together in the comfort of our own homes. To build a bowl that showcases the bounty of an Italian harvest, we started with farro, an ancient Mediterranean wheat grain with a pleasant chew and nutty flavor. For our Italian farmers' market–fresh vegetables, we loved the contrast of bitter radicchio alongside sweet roasted butternut squash. Ripe figs gave our harvest bowl a honey-like and slightly nutty flavor. A scant ¼ cup of blue cheese on top lent just enough pungency to balance out the sweet and bitter ingredients. As a finishing touch we whipped together a quick and simple balsamic vinaigrette, emulsified with sharp Dijon mustard. Any type of fresh fig will work in this recipe.

2 tablespoons balsamic vinegar
1 teaspoon Dijon mustard
¼ teaspoon table salt
¼ teaspoon pepper
3 tablespoons extra-virgin olive oil
2 cups cooked farro (page 189)

½ head radicchio (5 ounces), cored and cut into 1-inch pieces
¼ cup fresh parsley leaves
1 cup Roasted Butternut Squash (page 203)
4 fresh figs, halved and sliced thin
¼ cup crumbled blue cheese

Whisk vinegar, mustard, salt, and pepper together in bowl. While whisking constantly, slowly drizzle in oil until combined. Toss farro, radicchio, and parsley with half of vinaigrette to coat then season with salt and pepper to taste. Divide among individual serving bowls then top with roasted squash, figs, and blue cheese. Drizzle with remaining vinaigrette. Serve.

■ **CUSTOMIZE IT**

For extra crunch	Add a handful of chopped walnuts.
Simplify the dressing	Use a store-bought balsamic vinaigrette (you'll want about ⅓ cup).
Instead of radicchio	Endive would work here.
Instead of fresh figs	Use a sliced pear.

Farro Bowl with Tofu, Mushrooms, and Spinach

Serves 2 | Calories per Serving: 680

Why This Recipe Works   We love that vegetable-and-grain bowls give you the freedom to mix things up—literally and stylistically—at dinnertime. This bowl is a shining example of that. Hearty and nutty farro, the base, is often associated with Italy and flavor profiles of the western Mediterranean, but for a new take we thought it would stand up well to bold Asian ingredients. For toppings, we chose crispy seared tofu planks, along with a simple sauté of mushrooms, shallot, and spinach. We partnered these easy-to-prepare toppings with a potent miso-ginger sauce, which is enhanced with a little mayo for body so it's the perfect drizzle-able consistency.

7 ounces firm tofu, sliced crosswise into 4 equal slabs

⅛ teaspoon plus pinch table salt, divided

⅛ teaspoon pepper

3 tablespoons cornstarch

2 tablespoons vegetable oil, divided

5 ounces cremini mushrooms, trimmed and chopped coarse

1 tablespoon minced shallot

1 tablespoon dry sherry

5 ounces (5 cups) baby spinach

2 cups cooked farro (page 189), warmed

1 teaspoon toasted sesame oil

½ teaspoon sherry vinegar

¼ cup Miso-Ginger Sauce (page 221)

2 scallions, sliced thin

1. Spread tofu over paper towel–lined plate, let drain for 20 minutes, then gently press dry with paper towels. Sprinkle with ⅛ teaspoon salt and pepper.

2. Gently toss drained tofu with cornstarch in bowl. Heat 1 tablespoon vegetable oil in 12-inch nonstick skillet over medium-high heat until shimmering. Add tofu and brown lightly on all sides, 12 to 15 minutes; transfer to clean paper towel–lined plate to drain.

3. In now-empty skillet, heat 2 teaspoons vegetable oil over medium-high heat until shimmering. Stir in mushrooms, shallot, and remaining pinch salt and cook until vegetables begin to brown, 5 to 8 minutes. Stir in sherry and cook, scraping up any browned bits, until skillet is nearly dry, about 1 minute; transfer to bowl. Heat remaining 1 teaspoon vegetable oil over medium-high heat in again-empty skillet until shimmering. Add spinach, 1 handful at a time, and cook until just wilted, about 1 minute.

4. Toss farro with sesame oil and vinegar then season with salt and pepper to taste. Divide among individual bowls then top with tofu, mushrooms, and spinach. Drizzle with miso-ginger sauce, sprinkle with scallions, and serve.

■ **CUSTOMIZE IT**

Instead of farro	Try quinoa, barley, or brown rice (see pages 189–192).
Simplify the dressing	Use store-bought ginger dressing.

Chimichurri Couscous Bowl

Serves 2 | Calories per Serving: 710

Why This Recipe Works Bold, bright chimichurri sauce highlights the incredible flavor of fresh parsley and comes together in a snap. Chimichurri is often served over beef, but instead we were inspired by the equally parsley-forward flavor of tabbouleh. We used the sauce to add bright flavor and color to a base of pearl couscous, which had the perfect hearty texture to hold its own with the bold sauce. For protein, instead of beef, we crumbled tofu before crisping it on the stovetop with garlic. Hefty portions of parsley on top of our herb-forward chimichurri added pleasant vegetal flavors, and cucumber added cool crispness. Sun-dried tomatoes rounded out our flavor profile. Use vegetable broth instead of chicken broth to make this dish vegan.

- 7 ounces firm tofu, crumbled into ¼- to ½-inch pieces
- ⅛ teaspoon table salt
- ⅛ teaspoon pepper
- 4½ teaspoons extra-virgin olive oil, divided
- 1 cup pearl couscous
- 1¼ cups chicken or vegetable broth
- 1 garlic clove, minced
- ½ cup chopped fresh parsley
- ¼ cup Chimichurri Sauce (page 223), divided
- ½ English cucumber, chopped fine
- ¼ cup oil-packed sun-dried tomatoes, rinsed, patted dry, and chopped fine

1. Spread tofu over paper towel–lined plate, let drain for 20 minutes, then gently press dry with paper towels. Sprinkle with salt and pepper.

2. Meanwhile, cook 2 teaspoons oil and couscous in medium saucepan over medium heat, stirring frequently, until half of grains are golden brown, about 3 minutes. Stir in broth and bring to boil. Reduce heat to medium-low, cover, and simmer, stirring occasionally, until couscous is tender and broth is absorbed, 9 to 12 minutes.

3. Remove couscous from heat and let sit, covered, for 3 minutes. Transfer to bowl to cool slightly, about 10 minutes.

4. While couscous cools, heat 2 teaspoons oil in 12-inch nonstick skillet over medium-high heat until shimmering. Add tofu and cook, stirring occasionally, until lightly browned, 6 to 8 minutes. Push tofu to sides of skillet. Add remaining ½ teaspoon oil and garlic to center and cook, mashing garlic into skillet, until fragrant, about 30 seconds. Stir mixture into tofu and remove skillet from heat.

5. Stir parsley and 2 tablespoons chimichurri sauce into cooled couscous in bowl and season with salt and pepper to taste. Divide evenly among individual serving bowls then top with tofu, cucumber, and sun-dried tomatoes. Drizzle with remaining chimichurri sauce. Serve.

▧ CUSTOMIZE IT

Instead of sun-dried tomatoes	Use 4 ounces fresh cherry tomatoes, quartered.
Instead of cucumber	Try 1 rib thinly sliced celery.
Make it meaty	Use cooked chicken instead of tofu.
Kick it up a notch	Substitute chopped mint for some of the parsley.

Smoked Trout and Couscous Bowl

Serves 2 | Calories per Serving: 650

Why This Recipe Works Smoked trout often plays second fiddle to smoked salmon, but it really shouldn't. It offers an umami-dense salty bite, just the right amount of smoke, and the same convenience: Open the package and serve. We made a cohesive topping out of the flaked trout by mixing it with a little crème fraîche, chives, and lemon zest and juice—all of which complemented the smoky flavor without overwhelming it. For the base of our bowl, we chose pearl couscous, which has a pleasant chewy texture and toasty flavor. Radish added crisp freshness, which kept the bowl bright and light. To tie everything together, we made a quick vinaigrette featuring smoked paprika, which we tossed with the couscous and drizzled over the top for maximum flavor in every bite. You can substitute sour cream for the crème fraîche, though the trout mixture will be tangier. You can substitute red wine vinegar for the sherry vinegar.

3 ounces smoked trout, skin removed, flaked into ½-inch pieces

3 tablespoons crème fraîche

2 tablespoons minced fresh chives

½ teaspoon grated lemon zest plus ½ teaspoon juice, plus lemon wedges for serving

2 tablespoons extra-virgin olive oil, divided

1 cup pearl couscous

1¼ cups chicken or vegetable broth

2 teaspoons sherry vinegar

½ teaspoon Dijon mustard

½ teaspoon smoked paprika

⅛ teaspoon table salt

2 radishes, trimmed and cut into matchsticks

1. Combine smoked trout, crème fraîche, chives, and lemon zest and juice in bowl and season with pepper to taste; set aside until ready to serve.

2. Cook 2 teaspoons oil and couscous in medium saucepan over medium heat, stirring frequently, until half of grains are golden brown, about 3 minutes. Stir in broth and bring to boil. Reduce heat to medium-low, cover, and simmer, stirring occasionally, until couscous is tender and broth is absorbed, 9 to 12 minutes. Remove couscous from heat and let sit, covered, for 3 minutes. Transfer to bowl to cool slightly, about 10 minutes.

3. Whisk vinegar, mustard, paprika, and salt together in separate bowl. While whisking constantly, slowly drizzle in remaining 4 teaspoons oil until combined. Toss couscous with 1 tablespoon vinaigrette to coat then season with salt and pepper to taste. Divide among individual serving bowls then top with radishes and smoked trout mixture. Drizzle with remaining vinaigrette. Serve.

■ **CUSTOMIZE IT**

Add some greens	Try watercress, arugula, or other leafy greens.
For extra crunch	Top with toasted, chopped walnuts.
Make it spicy	Add a pinch (or more) of cayenne pepper to the vinaigrette.
Instead of trout	You can use smoked salmon.

Thanksgiving Quinoa Bowl

Serves 2 | Calories per Serving: 600

Why This Recipe Works Turkey, stuffing, green beans: Thanksgiving is usually an all-day culinary affair, but there's no need to thaw a whole turkey here. Instead, we made mini turkey meatballs, packed full of iconic stuffing spices like fennel and sage and easily browned in a skillet. We bypassed heavy mashed potatoes for quinoa, which is not only good for you, but also acts as a binder for the bowl components, making it easier to get a little of everything in each bite. For the easiest-ever green beans, we gave them a quick sauté in a skillet. Our meatballs were so tender they didn't need the help of thick gravy, but for homey flavor we drizzled our Creamy Roasted Garlic Dressing over the top. Dried cranberries added a pop of sweetness—and a nod to cranberry sauce. Be sure to use ground turkey in this recipe, not ground turkey breast (also labeled 99 percent fat-free).

½ slice hearty white sandwich bread, crust removed, torn into ¼-inch pieces
1 tablespoon milk
8 ounces ground turkey
2 tablespoons chopped fresh parsley
¾ teaspoon ground fennel
¾ teaspoon ground sage
¼ teaspoon plus pinch table salt, divided
¼ teaspoon pepper

2 teaspoons vegetable oil, divided
4 ounces green beans, trimmed and halved crosswise
2 cups cooked quinoa (page 192), warmed
2 tablespoons Creamy Roasted Garlic Dressing (page 224)
2 tablespoons dried cranberries

1. Mash bread and milk into paste in medium bowl using fork. Break turkey into small pieces over bread mixture and add parsley, fennel, sage, ¼ teaspoon salt, and pepper. Lightly knead with hands until well combined. Pinch off and roll mixture into 18 meatballs (about ½ tablespoon each).

2. Heat 1 teaspoon oil in 12-inch nonstick skillet over medium heat until shimmering. Add meatballs and cook until well browned and tender, 5 to 7 minutes. Transfer meatballs to plate, cover with aluminum foil to keep warm, and set aside until ready to serve. Heat remaining 1 teaspoon oil in now-empty skillet over medium-high heat until shimmering. Add green beans and remaining pinch salt and cook until green beans are spotty brown, 2 to 4 minutes.

3. Divide quinoa among individual serving bowls then top with meatballs and green beans. Drizzle with dressing and sprinkle with cranberries. Serve.

■ **CUSTOMIZE IT**

Kick it up a notch	Add Crispy Shallots (page 212), or use store-bought French's crispy onions in a pinch.
Simplify the dressing	Use store-bought roasted garlic dressing.

Pork Mojo Quinoa Bowl

Why This Recipe Works Pork *mojo*, a Cuban staple, is all about infusing slow-cooked pork with a citrusy, garlicky mojo sauce made from sour oranges. It's often served over rice, so we knew the flavors of pork mojo would make for a perfect bowl, but we needed to stream-line the cooking process to make it more weeknight-friendly. Pork shoulder, the traditional cut, takes hours to braise and is fatty, but we found that quick-cooking lean pork tenderloin turned it meltingly tender enough to shred using two forks (see page 195). Instead of hard-to-find sour oranges, we used a combination of orange and lime juice, as well as orange zest. To take the raw edge off the garlic, we quickly microwaved it in extra-virgin olive oil. Cumin and oregano added deep flavor, and a combination of bell pepper, poblano, and pickled jalapeños, along with some cut-up orange, created a unique topping with texture and spice. Rather than protein-lacking rice, we served our flavorful pork over a bed of hearty quinoa.

2 oranges (1 orange grated and juiced to get ½ teaspoon zest and ¼ cup juice, 1 orange left whole)

1 small red bell pepper, stemmed, seeded, and cut into ¼-inch pieces

1 small poblano pepper, stemmed, seeded, and cut into ¼-inch pieces

2 tablespoons pickled jalapeños, minced

2 tablespoons extra-virgin olive oil

2 garlic cloves, minced

¾ teaspoon ground cumin

¼ cup lime juice (2 limes)

1½ teaspoons minced fresh oregano

2 cups cooked quinoa (page 192), warmed

1 recipe Roast Pork Tenderloin (page 195), shredded and warmed

3 tablespoons chopped fresh cilantro

1. Cut away peel and pith from whole orange. Quarter orange, then slice crosswise ½ inch thick. Combine orange pieces, bell pepper, poblano, and pickled jalapeños in bowl and season with salt and pepper to taste; set aside until ready to serve.

2. Microwave oil, garlic, and cumin in medium bowl until fragrant, about 1 minute. Whisk orange zest and juice, lime juice, and oregano into oil mixture. Toss quinoa with ⅓ cup vinaigrette and season with salt and pepper to taste. Toss pork with remaining vinaigrette and season with salt and pepper to taste. Divide quinoa among individual serving bowls then top with pork and orange–bell pepper mixture. Sprinkle with cilantro. Serve.

■ **CUSTOMIZE IT**

Make it creamy	Add a dollop of sour cream.
For extra crunch	Top with plantain chips.
Instead of quinoa	Try brown rice or bulgur (page 189).

Egyptian Barley Bowl

Serves 2 | Calories per Serving: 580

Why This Recipe Works We set out to develop a recipe for a vibrantly spiced pearl barley salad with the right balance of sweetness, earthiness, tang, and nuttiness. Inspired by the flavors of Egypt, we incorporated toasty pistachios, tangy pomegranate molasses, and bright, vegetal cilantro, all balanced by warm, earthy spices and sweet golden raisins. We bulked it up with our marinated eggplant, a topping you can make ahead and keep on hand. This often bitter vegetable gets the broiler treatment, giving it lots of caramelization, and then gets tossed in a bright vinaigrette full of capers and mint. Salty feta cheese, pungent scallions, and pomegranate seeds adorned the top of the dish for a colorful composed salad with dynamic flavors and textures. Chopped pistachios added both crunch and color. We like this bowl served warm or room temperature.

- 2 tablespoons extra-virgin olive oil
- 1 tablespoon pomegranate molasses
- ¼ teaspoon ground cinnamon
- ¼ teaspoon table salt
- ¼ teaspoon pepper
- ⅛ teaspoon ground cumin
- 2 cups cooked pearl barley (page 189)
- ¼ cup chopped fresh cilantro
- 2 tablespoons golden raisins
- ¾ cup Marinated Eggplant with Capers and Mint (page 206), chopped coarse
- 1 ounce feta cheese, crumbled (¼ cup)
- ¼ cup pomegranate seeds
- 3 scallions, green parts only, sliced thin
- 2 tablespoons chopped toasted pistachios

Whisk oil, pomegranate molasses, cinnamon, salt, pepper, and cumin together in bowl. Toss barley, cilantro, and raisins with 1 tablespoon vinaigrette to coat then season with salt and pepper to taste. Divide among individual serving bowls then top with eggplant, feta, pomegranate seeds, and scallion greens. Drizzle with remaining vinaigrette and sprinkle with pistachios. Serve.

■ CUSTOMIZE IT

Make it vegan	Omit the feta.
Kick it up a notch	Top with Pistachio Dukkah (page 211) instead of pistachios.
Instead of barley	Try white rice or bulgur (page 189).
For extra protein	Add shredded chicken (page 194).

Turkey Meatball and Barley Bowl

Serves 2 | Calories per Serving: 620

For more information on arranging toppings, see pages 12–13.

Why This Recipe Works If you're looking to up your weeknight rotation, look no further. Using just a handful of pantry staples, we built a bowl filled with warm spices and exciting flavors that was still simple enough to throw together after a long workday. Ground turkey with an easy white bread panade made for tender, quick-cooking meatballs spiced with cumin, paprika, and cilantro. Making the most of our spice rack, we gave carrots and snow peas a dusting of cumin and cooked them in the same skillet we used for the meatballs to minimize cleanup. Hearty, chewy barley made for the perfect base with a nuttiness that's hard to beat, so we kept the dressing simple with some oil, lemon, and cilantro. Be sure to use ground turkey in this recipe, not ground turkey breast (also labeled 99 percent fat-free). For more information on arranging toppings, see pages 12–13.

½ slice hearty white sandwich bread, crust removed, torn into ¼-inch pieces

1 tablespoon milk

8 ounces ground turkey

¼ cup chopped fresh cilantro, divided

1 teaspoon ground cumin, divided

¾ teaspoon paprika

¼ teaspoon table salt, divided

¼ teaspoon pepper

2 tablespoons plus 1 teaspoon extra-virgin olive oil, divided

3 carrots, peeled

4 ounces snow peas, strings removed, halved lengthwise

1 teaspoon grated lemon zest plus 1 tablespoon juice

2 cups cooked barley (page 189), warmed

¼ cup plain Greek yogurt

1. Mash bread and milk into paste in medium bowl using fork. Break turkey into small pieces over bread mixture and add 2 tablespoons cilantro, ¾ teaspoon cumin, paprika, ⅛ teaspoon salt, and pepper. Lightly knead with hands until well combined. Pinch off and roll mixture into 18 meatballs (about ½ tablespoon each).

2. Heat 1 teaspoon oil in 12-inch nonstick skillet over medium heat until shimmering. Add meatballs and cook until well browned and tender, 5 to 7 minutes. Transfer meatballs to plate, cover with aluminum foil to keep warm, and set aside until ready to serve.

3. Halve carrots crosswise, then halve or quarter lengthwise to create uniformly sized pieces. Heat 1 tablespoon oil in now-empty skillet over medium heat until shimmering. Add carrots, remaining ¼ teaspoon cumin, and remaining ⅛ teaspoon salt and cook, stirring occasionally, until lightly charred and just tender, 5 to 7 minutes. Stir in snow peas and cook until crisp-tender, 2 to 4 minutes; set aside off heat.

4. Whisk remaining 1 tablespoon oil, remaining 2 tablespoons cilantro, and lemon zest and juice together in large bowl. Add barley, tossing to coat, then season with salt and pepper to taste. Divide among individual serving bowls then top with meatballs and carrot mixture. Dollop with yogurt. Serve.

■ CUSTOMIZE IT

Kick it up a notch	Use Beet Tzatziki (page 226) instead of Greek yogurt. Add Quick Sweet and Spicy Pickled Red Onions (page 217) and/or a handful of Spiced Pepitas or Sunflower Seeds (page 210). Add microgreens for color and freshness.
For extra crunch	Add quartered raw radishes.

Golden Bulgur Bowl

Serves 2 | Calories per Serving: 650

Why This Recipe Works Inspired by the bright, bold flavors of Middle Eastern pilaf, we paired floral bulgur with savory turkey sausage and a saffron-infused pomegranate vinaigrette, which added outstanding flavor and turned our bowl a gorgeous gold color. Dried apricots, cooked with savory fennel and a little water to help plump the apricots, added contrasting texture and pleasant sweetness. We tossed the bulgur with some of the saffron vinaigrette, which emphasized the bulgur's golden tint, then topped it with sausage and our fennel-apricot mixture. A little shaved Manchego was the cherry on top. When shopping, don't confuse bulgur with cracked wheat, which has a much longer cooking time and will not work in this recipe. You will need a 12-inch nonstick skillet with a tight-fitting lid.

2 tablespoons extra-virgin olive oil, divided
8 ounces turkey Italian sausage
1 fennel bulb, 2 tablespoons fronds minced, stalks discarded, bulb halved, cored, and sliced ¼ inch thick
¼ cup dried apricots, chopped
¼ cup plus 1 teaspoon hot water, divided

¼ teaspoon table salt, divided
¼ teaspoon pepper, divided
⅛ teaspoon saffron threads, crumbled
1 tablespoon pomegranate molasses
½ teaspoon grated lemon zest
2 cups cooked bulgur (page 189), warmed
1 ounce Manchego cheese, shaved

1. Heat 1 tablespoon oil in 12-inch nonstick skillet over medium heat until shimmering. Add sausage and cook until browned on all sides and registers 160 degrees, 6 to 8 minutes. Transfer to cutting board, cover with aluminum foil, and let rest. Slice sausage ½ inch thick on bias before serving.

2. Pour off all but 2 teaspoons fat from skillet (or add oil to equal 2 teaspoons). Add sliced fennel, apricots, ¼ cup water, ⅛ teaspoon salt, and ⅛ teaspoon pepper, cover, and cook over medium heat for 1 minute. Uncover and continue to cook, stirring occasionally, until fennel is spotty brown, 2 to 4 minutes; set aside until ready to serve.

3. Combine saffron with remaining 1 teaspoon water in large bowl and let sit for 5 minutes. Whisk remaining 1 tablespoon oil, remaining ⅛ teaspoon salt, remaining ⅛ teaspoon pepper, pomegranate molasses, and lemon zest into saffron mixture, then stir in bulgur to coat. Divide among individual serving bowls, then top with fennel mixture and sausage. Sprinkle with fennel fronds and Manchego cheese. Serve.

■ **CUSTOMIZE IT**

For extra crunch	Add toasted pine nuts.
Make it vegan	Use Pan-Seared Tofu (page 198) instead of sausage and omit Manchego.
Instead of Manchego	Use shaved Parmesan.

Bulgur, Pork, and Pesto Bowl

Serves 2 | Calories per Serving: 660

Why This Recipe Works Pork tenderloin is lean and tender and cooks up quickly, making it the perfect starting point for an easy weeknight bowl. We wanted to coax its subtle flavor out by pairing it with complementary, not overpowering, flavors. After coating the pork with an abundant amount of ground fennel, we seared it for flavorful browning before finishing it gently in the oven. Meanwhile, we reused our skillet to cook up some asparagus and red bell pepper. Quick-cooking bulgur made a particularly good accompaniment to the tenderloin: We tossed the cooked bulgur with some olive oil and lemon zest to bring out its natural herby and floral flavors. Convenient store-bought pesto added a flavorful punch (you can use basil pesto, or any other variety you like), while pickled grapes, an easily made-ahead item, added pleasant tart-sweetness. Thin the pesto with hot water as needed before drizzling.

- 1 (12-ounce) pork tenderloin, trimmed
- 2 teaspoons ground fennel
- ½ teaspoon table salt, divided
- ½ teaspoon pepper, divided
- 2 tablespoons extra-virgin olive oil, divided
- 6 ounces asparagus, trimmed and cut into 2-inch lengths on bias

- 1 red bell pepper, stemmed, seeded, and sliced thin
- 2 tablespoons water
- 2 cups cooked bulgur (page 189), warmed
- ½ teaspoon grated lemon zest
- ¼ cup pesto
- ½ cup Quick Pickled Grapes (page 216)

1. Adjust oven rack to lower-middle position and heat oven to 450 degrees. Pat tenderloin dry with paper towels and sprinkle with ground fennel, ¼ teaspoon salt, and ¼ teaspoon pepper. Heat 2 teaspoons oil in 12-inch ovensafe skillet over medium-high heat until just smoking. Brown tenderloin on all sides, about 10 minutes. Remove tenderloin and wipe out skillet.

2. Transfer tenderloin to 8-inch square baking dish and roast until meat registers 135 degrees, 10 to 15 minutes, flipping tenderloin halfway through roasting. Transfer tenderloin to carving board, tent with aluminum foil, and let rest. Slice tenderloin thin before serving.

3. Meanwhile, heat 1 teaspoon oil in now-empty skillet over medium heat until shimmering. Add asparagus, bell pepper, water, remaining ¼ teaspoon salt, and remaining ¼ teaspoon pepper, cover, and cook for 2 minutes. Uncover and continue to cook, stirring occasionally, until vegetables are crisp-tender, about 2 minutes.

4. Toss bulgur with remaining 1 tablespoon oil and lemon zest to coat then season with salt and pepper to taste. Divide among individual serving bowls then top with asparagus mixture and tenderloin. Drizzle with pesto (thinning pesto with hot water as needed) and sprinkle with grapes. Serve.

■ **CUSTOMIZE IT**

Instead of asparagus	Substitute Sautéed Broccoli with Garlic and Thyme (page 203) or Roasted Carrots (page 205).
Instead of grapes	Top with orange or grapefruit segments.

Shredded Pork and Pinto Bean Tostada Bowl

Serves 2 | Calories per Serving: 680

Why This Recipe Works The flavors of tostadas—spicy sauce, tender pork, and a crunchy tortilla—are unbeatable, so for a bowl packed with spicy heat and tender meat, we deconstructed the tostada. Shredded pork tenderloin and spicy chile sauce mixed with a hearty pinto bean base gave us complex flavor. Crunchy tortilla chips on top mimicked the flat, fried tortilla of traditional tostadas, and a quick radish and jícama slaw gave us bright, bold flavor and crunch. Use the large holes of a box grater to shred the jícama.

4 ounces jícama, peeled and shredded (1 cup)

2 radishes, trimmed, halved, and sliced thin

4 teaspoons extra-virgin olive oil, divided

½ teaspoon grated lime zest plus 2 teaspoons juice, plus lime wedges for serving

1 small onion, chopped fine

4 garlic cloves, minced

2 teaspoons chili powder

2 teaspoons minced canned chipotle chile in adobo sauce

1½ teaspoons ground cumin

1 cup canned tomato sauce

1 recipe Roast Pork Tenderloin (page 195), shredded

1 (15-ounce) can pinto beans, rinsed

1 ounce tortilla chips, broken into bite-size pieces (1 cup)

½ ripe avocado, sliced

¼ cup chopped fresh cilantro

1. Combine jícama, radishes, 1 teaspoon oil, and lime zest and juice in bowl and season with salt and pepper to taste; set aside until ready to serve.

2. Heat remaining 1 tablespoon oil in 12-inch nonstick skillet over medium heat until shimmering. Add onion and cook until softened, about 5 minutes. Stir in garlic, chili powder, chipotle chile in adobo, and cumin and cook until fragrant, about 30 seconds. Stir in tomato sauce and simmer gently until flavors meld, about 3 minutes. Stir in tenderloin and beans and cook, stirring occasionally, until tenderloin is warmed through, about 2 minutes. Season with salt and pepper to taste and adjust consistency with hot water as needed.

3. Divide pork mixture among individual serving bowls, then top with jícama mixture, tortilla chips, and avocado. Sprinkle with cilantro. Serve with lime wedges.

■ **CUSTOMIZE IT**

Kick it up a notch	Add crumbled *queso fresco* or a splash of hot sauce.
Instead of pinto beans	Try black beans.

Shakshuka Bowl

Serves 2 | Calories per Serving: 470

Why This Recipe Works   Shakshuka, the new "it" Sunday brunch menu item, features eggs poached in a tomato sauce flavored with peppers, garlic, and Middle Eastern spices. For our at-home sauce we started with pantry spices—lemony coriander, hot smoked paprika, warm cumin, and zesty pepper flakes. After blooming our spices and garlic in oil, we added crushed tomatoes along with a can of rinsed cannellini beans. Though not typical of a classic shakshuka, we found that the beans not only bulked up our final dish, but helped to thicken the sauce, leaving a sturdy bed to poach our eggs in. To ensure that the eggs cooked just right, we added them to the skillet off heat and covered the whites' edges with some of our sauce to help speed up cooking. Covering the eggs created a steamy environment that quickly cooked them from above and below. Serve with a piece of hearty bread and enjoy the bowl for breakfast, lunch, brunch, or dinner. You will need a 28-ounce can for the 2 cups of crushed tomatoes and a 12-inch skillet with a tight-fitting lid for this recipe.

2 tablespoons extra-virgin olive oil	2 cups canned crushed tomatoes
2 garlic cloves, sliced thin	1 (15-ounce) can cannellini beans, rinsed
1½ teaspoons tomato paste	1 cup Roasted Bell Peppers (page 207), chopped
1 teaspoon ground coriander	
1 teaspoon hot smoked paprika	2 large eggs
½ teaspoon ground cumin	1 ounce feta cheese, crumbled (¼ cup)
¼ teaspoon red pepper flakes	2 tablespoons chopped fresh mint

1. Heat oil in 12-inch skillet over medium heat until shimmering. Add garlic, tomato paste, coriander, paprika, cumin, and pepper flakes and cook, stirring constantly, until rust-colored and fragrant, about 1 minute. Stir in tomatoes, beans, and roasted red peppers and bring to simmer. Cook, stirring occasionally, until warmed through, about 2 minutes.

2. Off heat, using back of spoon, make 2 shallow indentations in sauce. Crack 1 egg into each indentation then spoon sauce over edges of egg whites so that whites are partially covered and yolks are exposed. Bring to simmer over medium heat, cover, and cook until yolks film over and whites are softly but uniformly set, 4 to 6 minutes. Divide among individual serving bowls, then sprinkle with feta and mint. Serve.

■ **CUSTOMIZE IT**

Simplify the peppers	Use jarred roasted red peppers.
For crunch	Serve with crusty bread, Pita Crumble (page 214), or Croutons (page 215).
Add more herbs	Cilantro, chives, and parsley would make great additions to the mint.

Pantry Chickpea Bowl

Serves 2 | Calories per Serving: 390

Why This Recipe Works A meal that doesn't require a trip to the grocery store can be a lifesaver, let alone one that can be thrown together in less than thirty minutes. We wanted to come up with a bowl that was super pantry-friendly for those days when a speedy but healthy meal is a must. Baby spinach doesn't require much seasoning and takes just a few minutes to cook, making it the perfect starting point for our bowl. We cooked a little garlic in some olive oil until it just started to turn golden and added lots of spinach, one handful at a time, and let it wilt. Then we threw in a can of rinsed chickpeas (for protein and heft) and some sun-dried tomatoes (for sweetness to balance the savory base). Finally, we topped it off with a couple of fried eggs. With a dollop of lemony yogurt and some toasted pistachios, this bowl makes for a well-balanced, stress-free, and, most important, delicious meal for any night of the week.

¼ cup plain yogurt

¾ teaspoon grated lemon zest plus ½ teaspoon juice

1 tablespoon extra-virgin olive oil

2 garlic cloves, sliced thin

9 ounces (9 cups) baby spinach

1 (15-ounce) can chickpeas, rinsed

2 tablespoons oil-packed sun-dried tomatoes, rinsed, patted dry, and sliced thin

¼ teaspoon pepper

1 recipe Fried Eggs (page 199)

2 tablespoons chopped toasted pistachios

Combine yogurt and lemon zest and juice in bowl; set aside until ready to serve. Heat oil in 12-inch nonstick skillet over medium heat until shimmering. Add garlic and cook, stirring constantly, until light golden and beginning to sizzle, about 2 minutes. Add spinach, one handful at a time, and cook until wilted, about 1 minute. Stir in chickpeas, tomatoes, and pepper and cook until tomatoes are softened, 1 to 2 minutes; season with salt and pepper to taste. Divide among individual serving bowls then top with fried eggs. Drizzle with yogurt sauce and sprinkle with pistachios. Serve.

■ CUSTOMIZE IT

For extra crunch	Add Pistachio Dukkah (page 211), Savory Seed Brittle (page 211), or Frico Crumble (page 214).
Kick it up a notch	Use Tahini-Yogurt Sauce (page 226) instead of the lemon yogurt sauce.
Make it heartier	Serve with crusty bread.

Polenta Bowl with Broccoli Rabe and Fried Eggs

Serves 2 | Calories per Serving: 420

Why This Recipe Works Creamy, hearty polenta makes for a delicious and versatile base to any bowl, but can often end up gummy or rubbery, and achieving a porridge-like texture can take over an hour. To cut the time in half, we added just a pinch of baking soda, which lends an irresistible creamy consistency. Although polenta is often topped with a hearty ragu or robust tomato sauce, we wanted to take a lighter approach with toppings that wouldn't make you feel weighed down. We also wanted a bowl that you could easily throw together in a pinch. Our vegetable of choice was broccoli rabe, which has prominent nutty and bitter notes that set it apart from regular broccoli. We complemented the flavors with sautéed cherry tomatoes, which burst with sweet tomato flavor. For a protein boost and hint of decadence, we topped the whole thing off with a fried egg, so when we broke into the runny yolk it created its own irresistibly creamy sauce. You will need a 12-inch skillet with a tight-fitting lid for this recipe.

1 tablespoon extra-virgin olive oil

2 garlic cloves, minced

⅛ teaspoon table salt

⅛ teaspoon red pepper flakes

8 ounces broccoli rabe, trimmed and cut into 1½-inch pieces

2 tablespoons water

1 recipe Creamy Parmesan Polenta (page 192), warmed

¾ cup Sautéed Cherry Tomatoes (page 205), warmed

1 recipe Fried Eggs (page 199)

Heat oil in 12-inch nonstick skillet over medium-high heat until shimmering. Add garlic, salt, and pepper flakes and cook until fragrant, about 30 seconds. Stir in broccoli rabe and water, cover, and cook until broccoli rabe turns bright green, about 2 minutes. Uncover and cook, stirring frequently, until rabe is just tender, 2 to 3 minutes; season with salt and pepper to taste. Divide polenta among individual serving bowls then top with broccoli rabe, cherry tomatoes, and fried eggs. Serve.

▮ CUSTOMIZE IT

Kick it up a notch	Top with Frico Crumble (page 214) or Crispy Shallots (page 212).
Instead of broccoli rabe	Try Sautéed Broccoli with Garlic and Thyme (page 203).
For extra protein	Add Pan-Seared Flank Steak (page 195).

Shrimp and Grits Bowl

Serves 2 | Calories per Serving: 720

Why This Recipe Works A staple of the Southern table, grits are a great addition to any meal; we wanted to combine cheesy grits with plump shrimp for an easy weeknight dinner. We preferred quick grits to instant or old-fashioned for their creamy yet substantial texture. A mixture of broth and milk gave the grits a satisfying richness. Once the grits were cooked, we stirred in shredded cheddar cheese. For the shrimp, we found our Chipotle Shrimp to be a perfect fit for this recipe, but wanted something to drizzle over the top. While the grits cooked, we melted butter in a small skillet and bloomed additional chipotle chile powder. We drizzled this butter mixture over the top of our grits and shrimp, which added pleasant richness, spice, and smokiness to the composed dish. A sprinkle of bright scallion was a fresh finishing touch. Do not substitute instant grits or old-fashioned grits in this recipe.

½ cup fresh or frozen corn kernels
3 tablespoons unsalted butter, divided
1 small onion, chopped fine
1 garlic clove, minced
1½ cups chicken or vegetable broth
½ cup whole milk
½ cup quick grits

2 ounces extra-sharp cheddar cheese, shredded (½ cup)
¾ teaspoon chipotle chile powder
1 recipe Chipotle Shrimp (page 197), warmed
1 scallion, sliced thin

1. Microwave corn in bowl until tender, about 1 minute; set aside until ready to serve. Melt 1 tablespoon butter in medium saucepan over medium heat. Add onion and cook until softened, about 5 minutes. Stir in garlic and cook until fragrant, about 30 seconds. Stir in broth and milk and bring to simmer. Slowly whisk in grits, reduce heat to low, and cook, stirring often, until grits are thick and creamy, 5 to 7 minutes. Off heat, whisk in cheese then season with salt and pepper to taste; cover and set aside until ready to serve.

2. Melt remaining 2 tablespoons butter in 8-inch skillet over medium heat. Cook, swirling constantly, until butter is golden brown and has nutty aroma, about 2 minutes. Off heat, whisk in chipotle chile powder. Divide grits among individual serving bowls then top with shrimp, corn, and chipotle butter. Sprinkle with scallion. Serve.

■ **CUSTOMIZE IT**

Make it heartier	Add Sautéed Broccoli with Garlic and Thyme (page 203) or Sautéed Cherry Tomatoes (page 205).
Make it spicy	Add a thinly sliced jalapeño.

noodle bowls

Chicken Chow Mein Bowl

Serves 2 | Calories per Serving: 550

Why This Recipe Works When the craving for Chinese takeout strikes, this fast, fresh version of classic chow mein—a bowl packed with stir-fried chicken, vegetables, and noodles—is sure to satisfy. After cooking fresh Chinese noodles, we tossed them in a little oil to prevent them from clumping together. We then made a simple sauce and quickly cooked our chicken before adding shiitake mushrooms for their earthy umami flavor and carrots for a dose of necessary sweetness. Scallion greens added crunch and a pop of color. You can use any thin fresh Chinese egg noodle in this recipe; boil until just tender but still chewy.

¼ cup water
2 tablespoons oyster sauce
1 tablespoon soy sauce
1 teaspoon sugar
¼ teaspoon pepper
6 ounces fresh Chinese noodles
1 tablespoon toasted sesame oil
1 tablespoon vegetable oil

8 ounces boneless skinless chicken breasts, trimmed, halved lengthwise, and sliced thin crosswise
6 ounces shiitake mushrooms, stemmed and sliced thin
1 carrot, peeled and sliced thin on bias
3 scallions, white and green parts separated and sliced thin

1. Whisk water, oyster sauce, soy sauce, sugar, and pepper together in bowl; set sauce aside. Bring 2 quarts water to boil in large saucepan. Add noodles and cook, stirring often, until tender. Drain noodles and rinse thoroughly with cold water, shaking to remove excess water. Toss noodles with sesame oil in bowl and set aside until ready to serve.

2. Heat vegetable oil in 12-inch nonstick skillet over medium-high heat until just smoking. Add chicken in single layer and cook without stirring for 1 minute. Stir and continue to cook until lightly browned on both sides, about 1 minute longer. Add mushrooms and carrot and cook, stirring frequently, until vegetables are tender and mushrooms begin to brown, about 5 minutes. Stir in scallion whites and cook until fragrant, about 30 seconds. Off heat, stir in sauce.

3. Divide noodles among individual serving bowls then top with chicken mixture and sprinkle with scallion greens. Serve.

▦ CUSTOMIZE IT

For extra crunch	Sprinkle with chopped toasted cashews, bean sprouts, or Crispy Shallots (page 212).
Instead of fresh Chinese noodles	Substitute 6 ounces angel hair pasta.
Make it vegetarian	Double the amount of vegetables and omit the chicken.

Singapore Noodle Bowl

Serves 2 | Calories per Serving: 450

Why This Recipe Works Packed with curry flavor, stir-fried vegetables, and shrimp, Singapore-style noodles make for a perfect weeknight dinner. We swapped out the traditional, but delicate, rice vermicelli for resilient Chinese egg noodles, which held together during cooking. To develop complex flavor, we bloomed curry powder and aromatics in oil before adding soy sauce, sugar, and lime juice and tossing with the noodles. Sautéed carrots and red bell peppers, along with shrimp and cilantro, completed this speedy, satisfying dish. You can use any thin fresh Chinese egg noodle in this recipe; boil until just tender but still chewy. After preparing the Sautéed Shrimp, you can reuse the skillet for this recipe.

¼ cup water

2 teaspoons soy sauce

1½ teaspoons sugar

1 teaspoon lime juice, plus lime wedges for serving

6 ounces fresh Chinese noodles

4 teaspoons vegetable oil, divided

½ red bell pepper, sliced thin

1 small carrot, peeled and cut into 2-inch-long matchsticks

1 tablespoon curry powder

2 garlic cloves, minced

½ teaspoon grated fresh ginger

¾ cup Sautéed Shrimp (page 197), warmed

¼ cup fresh cilantro leaves

1 scallion, sliced thin on bias

1. Whisk water, soy sauce, sugar, and lime juice together in small bowl until sugar is dissolved; set aside. Bring 2 quarts water to boil in large saucepan. Add noodles and cook, stirring often, until nearly tender. Drain noodles and rinse thoroughly with cold water; set aside.

2. Heat 1 teaspoon oil in 12-inch nonstick skillet over medium heat until shimmering. Add bell pepper and carrot and cook, stirring frequently, until crisp-tender, about 2 minutes; transfer to bowl, cover with aluminum foil, and set aside until ready to serve.

3. Add remaining 1 tablespoon oil, curry powder, garlic, and ginger to now-empty skillet and cook over medium heat until fragrant, 15 to 30 seconds. Add soy sauce mixture and noodles, tossing to coat noodles with sauce, and cook until liquid is absorbed but noodles are still glossy, 1 to 2 minutes. Season with salt and pepper to taste. Divide among individual serving bowls, then top with vegetable mixture and shrimp and sprinkle with cilantro and scallions. Serve with lime wedges.

■ **CUSTOMIZE IT**

Make it vegetarian	Substitute Pan-Seared Tofu (page 198) for shrimp.
Kick it up a notch	Add cayenne pepper to the curry mixture or use a spicy curry powder.
Instead of fresh Chinese noodles	Substitute 6 ounces angel hair pasta.

Pork Lo Mein Bowl

Serves 2 | Calories per Serving: 650

Why This Recipe Works Lo mein is full of everything we love—seasoned noodles, seared pork, flavorful vegetables, and a salty-sweet sauce to coat. Rather than spend hours over barbecued pork, we opted for easy-to-cook tenderloin that we marinated in soy sauce, Chinese five-spice powder, and sesame oil. Quickly stir-frying our precooked noodles with scallions, ginger, garlic, and a spicy sauce allowed them to develop deep flavor in just a few seconds. For a finishing touch as beautiful as it is flavorful, we added baby bok choy, which we cooked to crisp-tender using a combination of searing and steaming. You can use any thin fresh Chinese egg noodle in this recipe; boil until just tender but still chewy.

- 1 teaspoon five-spice powder
- 1 teaspoon plus 1 tablespoon soy sauce, divided
- 2 teaspoons toasted sesame oil, divided
- 1 (12-ounce) pork tenderloin, trimmed and sliced thin
- 6 ounces fresh Chinese noodles
- 1½ tablespoons hoisin sauce

- 1 teaspoon chili-garlic sauce, plus extra for serving
- 2 tablespoons vegetable oil, divided
- 6 scallions, whites parts sliced thin, green parts cut into 1-inch pieces
- 1½ teaspoons grated fresh ginger
- 1 garlic clove, minced
- 2 heads baby bok choy (4 ounces each), halved

1. Whisk five-spice powder, 1 teaspoon soy sauce, and ½ teaspoon sesame oil together in medium bowl, then stir in pork to coat; let sit at room temperature for 15 minutes. Meanwhile, bring 2 quarts water to boil in large saucepan. Add noodles and cook, stirring often, until tender. Reserve ⅓ cup cooking water, drain noodles, and rinse thoroughly with cold water; set aside.

2. Whisk remaining 1 tablespoon soy sauce, remaining 1½ teaspoons sesame oil, hoisin, chili-garlic sauce, and reserved cooking water together in bowl. Heat 1 teaspoon vegetable oil in 12-inch nonstick skillet over medium-high heat until shimmering. Add cooked noodles, half of hoisin mixture, scallions, ginger, and garlic and cook until fragrant, about 30 seconds; season with salt and pepper to taste. Transfer to individual serving bowls, cover with aluminum foil to keep warm, and set aside until ready to serve.

3. Heat 1½ teaspoons vegetable oil in now-empty skillet over high heat until just smoking. Add half of pork and cook until browned on both sides, about 2 minutes; transfer to clean bowl. Repeat with 1½ teaspoons vegetable oil and remaining pork; transfer to clean bowl and cover with foil to keep warm.

4. Heat remaining 2 teaspoons oil in again-empty skillet over medium-high heat until just smoking. Add bok choy, cut side down, and 1 tablespoon water, cover, and cook until bok choy begins to brown, about 2 minutes. Flip bok choy and continue to cook, covered,

until second side is browned and bok choy is tender throughout, 1 to 2 minutes. Top noodles with pork and bok choy and drizzle with remaining sauce. Serve with extra chili garlic sauce.

■ **CUSTOMIZE IT**

Kick it up a notch	Toasted sesame seeds make a nice addition to this bowl.
Make it vegetarian	Substitute snap peas, broccoli, bell pepper, and/or mushrooms for the pork.
Instead of fresh Chinese noodles	Substitute 6 ounces angel hair pasta.

Summer Ramen Bowl

Serves 2 | **Calories per Serving: 530**

Why This Recipe Works A hot, steaming bowl of ramen noodles is the perfect fix on a cold, blustery day. But when the temperature rises, ramen noodles need a cooldown just as much as you do. Summer ramen—known as *hiyashi chuka* in Japan—are brothless ramen noodles tossed in a sweet-sour soy sauce dressing and served chilled with an array of toppings, providing textural contrast and visual appeal. While vegetables, eggs, and meat are most often found on the noodles, this dish presents a perfect opportunity for customizing based on what you have in the fridge or just brought home from the farmers' market. For our version, we tossed chilled ramen noodles with a soy sauce–based dressing perked up with rice vinegar, sesame oil, chili oil, and scallions. We topped the noodles with crisp cucumbers, rich avocado, and crunchy, spicy radishes. This elegant, summer-ready base is perfect for just about any protein, but we especially liked the combination of seafood and a hint of bright citrus. For a super-simple, no-cook topping, we tossed crab with both orange juice and zest, but you could use cooked shrimp or salmon instead. If using crab, be sure to purchase high-quality, fresh lump or jumbo lump crabmeat.

1 teaspoon vegetable oil

⅛ teaspoon grated orange zest plus 2 tablespoons juice

6 ounces lump crabmeat, picked over for shells and pressed dry between paper towels

2 (3-ounce) packages ramen noodles, seasoning packets discarded

3 tablespoons Sesame-Scallion Vinaigrette (page 220)

½ avocado, sliced thin

¼ English cucumber, cut into 2-inch-long matchsticks

2 radishes, trimmed, halved, and sliced thin

1 scallion, green part only, sliced thin on bias

1 teaspoon toasted sesame seeds

1. Whisk oil and orange zest and juice together in medium bowl. Add crabmeat, tossing to coat, then season with salt and pepper to taste; refrigerate until ready to serve.

2. Bring 2 quarts water to boil in large saucepan. Add noodles and cook, stirring frequently, until tender. Drain noodles in colander and rinse thoroughly with cold water, shaking to remove excess water. Toss noodles with vinaigrette and season with salt and pepper to taste. Divide among individual serving bowls then top with crabmeat mixture, avocado, cucumber, and radishes and sprinkle with scallion and sesame seeds. Serve.

■ **CUSTOMIZE IT**

Kick it up a notch | Serve with pickled ginger or crumbled nori, and top with herbs like cilantro or chives. Black sesame seeds add visual contrast.

Instead of crab | Use Sautéed Shrimp (page 197) or Oven-Roasted Salmon (page 197).

Yaki Udon Bowl

Serves 2 | Calories per Serving: 520

Why This Recipe Works For our version of Japanese *yaki udon*—a bowl of stir-fried udon noodles with vegetables and meat—we paired thick, chewy udon with juicy, browned beef and crisp-tender sautéed green beans. First, we marinated thinly sliced beef in oyster sauce, mirin, chili-garlic sauce, cornstarch (for clinging power), and sugar (for balance). To bring everything together, we created a quick sauce with flavors that mirrored the beef marinade and tossed it with our cooked noodles before assembling our bowl.

3 tablespoons oyster sauce, divided

2 teaspoons water

4 teaspoons mirin, divided

1½ teaspoons chili-garlic sauce, divided

½ teaspoon cornstarch

½ teaspoon sugar

8 ounces flank steak, trimmed, cut into 2-inch-wide strips with grain, and sliced thin crosswise

2 teaspoons vegetable oil

8 ounces fresh udon noodles

1 recipe Simple Sautéed Green Beans with Garlic (page 206), warmed

1 scallion, sliced thin

1. Whisk 1 tablespoon oyster sauce, water, 2 teaspoons mirin, ½ teaspoon chili-garlic sauce, cornstarch, and sugar together in medium bowl. Add beef, toss to coat, and set aside for 10 minutes.

2. Heat oil in 12-inch nonstick skillet over high heat until just smoking. Add beef in single layer and cook without stirring for 1 minute. Stir and continue to cook until spotty brown on both sides, about 1 minute longer; transfer to clean bowl.

3. Meanwhile, bring 2 quarts water to boil in large saucepan. Add udon noodles and cook, stirring often, until tender. Reserve ¼ cup cooking water, then drain noodles and return to pot. Whisk remaining 2 tablespoons oyster sauce, remaining 2 teaspoons mirin, and remaining 1 teaspoon chili-garlic sauce together then stir into noodles. Adjust consistency with reserved cooking water as needed and season with salt and pepper to taste. Divide among individual serving bowls then top with beef and green beans and sprinkle with scallion. Serve.

■ **CUSTOMIZE IT**

For extra crunch	Add bean sprouts.
Make it vegetarian	Use an Easy-Peel Soft-Cooked Egg (page 199) instead of steak—or use both.
Instead of mirin	Sweet sherry or white wine also work.
Instead of fresh udon	Substitute 6 ounces fresh Chinese noodles.
Instead of green beans	Sautéed Broccoli with Sesame Oil and Ginger (page 203) or Gingery Stir-Fried Edamame (page 198) would work.

Saucy Udon Noodle Bowl

Serves 2 | Calories per Serving: 350

Why This Recipe Works To create a vegetarian noodle dish that was delicate yet filling, we married the spicy bite of mustard greens with rustic udon noodles and a potent, broth-like sauce. Since udon noodles are starchy and a bit sweet, they stand up well to savory sauces, so we made a highly aromatic, flavorful sauce from Asian pantry staples: ginger, garlic, mirin, soy sauce, and chili-garlic sauce. After adding some reserved starchy pasta water (which we also used to wilt our greens), we achieved a sauce that was light and brothy but super-savory. To highlight the savoriness of the sauce, we added earthy sautéed mushrooms. Because fresh udon noodles cook so quickly, we made sure to add the greens to the pot before the noodles. Sesame seeds, sprinkled over the top of the bowl, added light crunch. Do not substitute other types of noodles for the udon noodles.

2 teaspoons vegetable oil
1 tablespoon grated fresh ginger
2 garlic cloves, minced
¼ cup mirin
1 tablespoon soy sauce
½ teaspoon chili-garlic sauce

8 ounces mustard greens, stemmed and cut into 2-inch pieces
8 ounces fresh udon noodles
1 cup Sautéed Mushrooms with Sesame and Ginger (page 207), warmed
¼ cup fresh cilantro leaves
1 tablespoon toasted sesame seeds

1. Heat oil in small saucepan over medium-high heat until shimmering. Add ginger and garlic and cook until fragrant, about 1 minute. Stir in mirin, soy sauce, and chili-garlic sauce and bring to brief simmer. Set aside off heat and cover to keep warm.

2. Bring 2 quarts water to boil in large saucepan. Add mustard greens and cook until leaves are nearly tender, about 3 minutes. Add udon noodles and cook, stirring often, until greens and noodles are tender, about 2 minutes. Reserve ¼ cup cooking water, then drain noodles and greens; divide among individual serving bowls. Stir reserved cooking water into mirin mixture then ladle evenly over noodles. Top with mushrooms and sprinkle with cilantro and sesame seeds. Serve.

▪ CUSTOMIZE IT

For extra protein	Top it off with Pan-Seared Tofu (page 198) or an Easy-Peel Soft-Cooked Egg (page 199).
Instead of mustard greens	Swiss chard works as a replacement.
Instead of mirin	Sweet sherry or white wine also work.

Bun Cha Noodle Bowl

Serves 2 | Calories per Serving: 600

Why This Recipe Works A traditional Vietnamese street food, *bun cha* combines flavorful pork patties with soft rice vermicelli, fragrant herbs, and the light yet potent Vietnamese sauce, *nuoc cham*. The vibrant contrast between salty, spicy, sweet, and sour flavors and soft, crispy, and crunchy textures makes this dish delectable, but thankfully not complicated or time consuming. Black pepper, shallot, and lime zest flavor the ground pork patties, and a test kitchen secret—baking soda—helps them stay juicy and brown quickly. Though they're often grilled, we quickly seared our patties. The nuoc cham sauce requires just a few ingredients, and the cooked patties are coated in the sauce before resting on a bed of noodles, cucumber slices, and carrot ribbons. A last drizzle of nuoc cham and a sprinkle of fresh mint is all you need to bring this Vietnamese specialty home. Do not substitute other types of noodles. A rasp-style grater makes quick work of turning the garlic into paste.

2 tablespoons fish sauce, divided
1 teaspoon grated lime zest plus
   4 teaspoons juice, plus lime wedges
   for serving
1 tablespoon plus ¾ teaspoon sugar,
   divided
½ Thai chile, stemmed and minced
1 small garlic clove, minced to paste
4 ounces rice vermicelli
1 small shallot, minced

¼ teaspoon pepper
¼ teaspoon baking soda
8 ounces ground pork
1 teaspoon vegetable oil
1 carrot, peeled and shaved into ribbons
   with vegetable peeler
¼ English cucumber, halved lengthwise,
   and sliced thin on bias
¼ cup torn fresh mint

1. Whisk ¼ cup hot water, 1½ tablespoons fish sauce, lime juice, 1 tablespoon sugar, Thai chile, and garlic together in medium bowl until sugar dissolves; set sauce aside. Bring 2 quarts water to boil in large saucepan. Off heat, add noodles and let sit until tender, about 5 minutes. Drain noodles and rinse with cold water until water runs clear, shaking to remove excess water.

2. Combine lime zest, shallot, pepper, baking soda, remaining 1½ teaspoons fish sauce, and remaining ¾ teaspoon sugar in medium bowl. Add pork and mix until well combined, then shape into 6 patties, each about 3 inches wide.

3. Heat oil in 12-inch skillet over medium-high heat until just smoking. Cook patties until well browned and meat registers 160 degrees, 2 to 4 minutes per side. Transfer patties to bowl with sauce and gently toss to coat. Let sit for 5 minutes.

4. Divide noodles among individual serving bowls, then top with carrot, cucumber, and patties. Drizzle remaining sauce over noodles and vegetables and sprinkle with mint. Serve with lime wedges.

■ CUSTOMIZE IT

Kick it up a notch	Add cilantro or basil for even more layers of flavor.
Instead of pork	Use ground turkey.
Instead of Thai chile	Use 1 teaspoon minced serrano chile or jalapeño.
For extra crunch	Use bean sprouts, snow peas, bell peppers, or whatever crunchy vegetable you have on hand in place of, or in addition to, the carrot and cucumber.
Add more greens	Replace each bowl with Bibb lettuce leaves to turn it into lettuce cups.

Shrimp Pad Thai Bowl

Serves 2 | Calories per Serving: 590

Why This Recipe Works We wanted a recipe for pad thai that cut the mile-long ingredient list without sacrificing authentic flavor. Soaking the rice noodles in just-boiled water ensured they remained loose and separate. For the requisite sweet, salty, sour, and spicy notes, we added sugar, fish sauce, rice vinegar, cayenne, lime juice, and dark brown sugar. Tender shrimp, lightly scrambled eggs, bean sprouts, and a sprinkling of scallion rounded out our streamlined pad thai. We prefer dark brown sugar here, but you can substitute light brown sugar. Do not substitute other types of noodles. This dish cooks very quickly; have everything prepared when you begin cooking.

3 tablespoons lime juice (2 limes)
2½ tablespoons packed dark brown sugar
2 tablespoons fish sauce
2½ tablespoons vegetable oil, divided
2 teaspoons rice vinegar
⅛ teaspoon cayenne pepper
4 ounces (¼-inch-wide) rice noodles
1 small shallot, minced

1 garlic clove, minced
  Pinch table salt
1 large egg, lightly beaten
2 scallions, green parts only,
  sliced thin, divided
¾ cup Sautéed Shrimp (page 197),
  warmed
2 ounces (1 cup) bean sprouts

1. Whisk lime juice, 3 tablespoons water, sugar, fish sauce, 1½ tablespoons oil, vinegar, and cayenne together in bowl; set aside. Pour 2 quarts boiling water over noodles in bowl and stir to separate. Let noodles soak until soft and pliable but not fully tender, stirring once halfway through soaking, 8 to 10 minutes. Drain noodles and rinse with cold water until water runs clear, shaking to remove excess water.

2. Heat remaining 1 tablespoon oil in 10-inch nonstick skillet over medium-high heat until shimmering. Add shallot, garlic, and salt and cook over medium heat, stirring constantly, until shallot is light golden brown, about 1½ minutes. Stir in egg and cook, stirring vigorously, until scrambled and barely moist, about 20 seconds.

3. Add drained rice noodles and toss to combine. Add lime mixture and half of scallions, increase heat to medium-high, and cook, tossing gently, until noodles are well coated and tender, about 3 minutes. (If not yet tender, add 2 tablespoons water to skillet and continue to cook until tender.) Season with salt and pepper to taste. Divide among individual serving bowls then top with shrimp and bean sprouts and sprinkle with remaining scallions. Serve.

■ **CUSTOMIZE IT**

| For extra crunch | Sprinkle with chopped unsalted dry-roasted peanuts. |
| Kick it up a notch | Sprinkle with cilantro and/or drizzle on Thai Chili Jam (page 221). |

Spicy Basil Noodle Bowl

Serves 2 | Calories per Serving: 530

Why This Recipe Works If you're looking for a dish to awaken your senses, these spicy basil rice noodles fit the bill. A potent sauce made from Thai chiles, shallots, garlic, lime juice, brown sugar, and fish sauce combines the intense flavors—hot, salty, sour, and sweet—that make Southeast Asian cooking distinct and irresistible. Quick-cooking baby bok choy, snap peas, and red bell peppers provide crunch and texture against the rice noodles, which are soaked in hot water to soften and then finish cooking in the feisty sauce. Pan-seared tofu provides "meatiness" without the meat. What puts this dish over the top, though, is an entire cup of Thai basil leaves tossed in with the noodles just before serving, adding aromatic notes of anise, cinnamon, and pepper. Reserving some fresh leaves to sprinkle on top lent a final hit of flavor. Do not substitute other types of noodles. You can substitute one jalapeño or serrano chile for the Thai chiles and an equal amount of regular basil for the Thai basil.

1 cup chicken or vegetable broth
2 tablespoons packed brown sugar
1½ tablespoons lime juice
1 tablespoon fish sauce
3 Thai chiles, stemmed, seeded, and chopped coarse
2 shallots, chopped coarse
3 garlic cloves, chopped coarse
4 ounces (⅜-inch-wide) rice noodles

1½ tablespoons vegetable oil, divided
2 heads baby bok choy (4 ounces each), sliced ¼ inch thick
½ red bell pepper, sliced thin
1 cup fresh Thai basil leaves, divided
1 cup Pan-Seared Tofu (page 198), warmed
1 ounce sugar snap peas, strings removed, sliced thin on bias

1. Whisk broth, sugar, lime juice, and fish sauce together in bowl until sugar dissolves; set aside. Process chiles, shallots, and garlic in blender, adding up to 3 tablespoons water and scraping down sides of blender jar as needed to form smooth paste, 15 to 20 seconds. Pour 2 quarts boiling water over noodles in bowl and stir to separate. Let noodles soak until soft and pliable but not fully tender, stirring once halfway through soaking, 12 to 15 minutes. Drain noodles and rinse with cold water until water runs clear, shaking to remove excess water.

2. Heat 1½ teaspoons oil in 12-inch nonstick skillet over high heat until shimmering. Add bok choy and bell pepper and cook until crisp-tender and lightly browned, 3 to 4 minutes; transfer to second bowl. Heat remaining 1 tablespoon oil in now-empty skillet over medium-high heat until shimmering. Add processed chile mixture and cook until color deepens, 3 to 5 minutes. Add noodles and broth mixture and cook, tossing gently, until noodles are well coated and tender, about 5 minutes. Season with salt and pepper to taste.

3. Stir ¾ cup basil leaves into noodles and cook until wilted, about 1 minute. Divide among individual serving bowls then top with browned vegetables, tofu, and snap peas. Tear remaining ¼ cup basil leaves over top. Serve.

■ CUSTOMIZE IT

Instead of bok choy	Substitute baby spinach and cook until wilted.
Instead of tofu	Try Sautéed Shrimp (page 197).
Make it vegan	Use Bragg Liquid Aminos in place of fish sauce.

Creamy Miso-Ginger Noodle Bowl

Serves 2 | **Calories per Serving: 500**

Why This Recipe Works A successful bowl combines an appealing assortment of flavors, colors, and textures. For a weeknight vegetarian noodle bowl that hit all the right notes and was easy to assemble, we started with rice noodles and added a savory miso-based sauce. Quickly marinating shredded carrots in seasoned rice vinegar added bright acidity and extra sweetness. Frozen edamame work straight from the freezer—a quick toss in a hot skillet keeps them crisp and fresh. Shredded red cabbage added crunch, and a sprinkle of herbs, sesame seeds, and lime juice kicked up the fresh flavors. You can use store-bought cole-slaw mix in place of the red cabbage. Do not substitute other types of noodles.

4 ounces (¼-inch-wide) rice noodles
1 carrot, peeled and shredded
1 tablespoon seasoned rice vinegar
1 teaspoon vegetable oil
½ cup frozen edamame
¾ cup water

½ cup Miso-Ginger Sauce (page 221)
½ cup shredded red cabbage
½ cup torn fresh cilantro
1 teaspoon toasted sesame seeds
Lime wedges

1. Pour 2 quarts boiling water over noodles in bowl and stir to separate. Let noodles soak until soft and pliable but not fully tender, stirring once halfway through soaking, 8 to 10 minutes. Drain noodles and rinse with cold water until water runs clear, shaking to remove excess water. Combine carrot and vinegar in bowl; set aside until ready to serve.

2. Heat oil in 12-inch nonstick skillet over medium-high heat until just smoking. Add edamame and cook until spotty brown but still bright green, about 2 minutes; transfer to second bowl. Combine noodles and water in now-empty skillet and cook until noodles are tender and water has been absorbed, 3 to 4 minutes. Off heat, stir in miso sauce and season with salt and pepper to taste.

3. Divide noodles among individual serving bowls then top with carrot, edamame, and cabbage and sprinkle with cilantro and sesame seeds. Serve with lime wedges.

■ **CUSTOMIZE IT**

Kick it up a notch	Substitute Quick Pickled Carrot Ribbons (page 217) for the shredded carrot. Add fresh mint along with the cilantro for extra herb flavor.
Instead of cabbage	Try bean sprouts, cucumber, or bell pepper.
Simplify the sauce	Use your favorite store-bought ginger dressing.
Make it meaty	Use shredded chicken instead of edamame.

Pork and Eggplant Soba Noodle Bowl with Miso

Serves 2 | Calories per Serving: 640

Why This Recipe Works Miso, a Japanese paste made from fermented soybeans (and sometimes grains), brings intense savory flavor to any dish and provides a complex balance of sweet, tart, and salty flavors. We knew that when combined with softened butter and scallions, white miso transforms into an earthy, umami-packed butter that melts into a decadent sauce when tossed with warm, starchy soba noodles. To the noodles we added golden-brown cubes of sautéed eggplant that had a creamy texture and mild flavor to complement the nutty noodles and potent sauce. We then browned ground pork until it was just crispy in spots to add texture, and seasoned it with soy sauce, ginger, garlic, and toasted sesame oil. A sprinkling of scallions added fresh flavor and color.

1½ tablespoons white miso
1½ tablespoons unsalted butter, softened
2 scallions (1 minced; 1 sliced thin on bias, green and white parts separated), divided
Pinch pepper
6 ounces soba noodles

1 tablespoon vegetable oil, divided
8 ounces eggplant, cut into ½-inch pieces
4 ounces ground pork
1 teaspoon soy sauce
1 garlic clove, minced
½ teaspoon grated fresh ginger
½ teaspoon toasted sesame oil

1. Mash miso, butter, minced scallion, and pepper together in medium bowl until homogeneous. Bring 2 quarts water to boil in large saucepan. Add noodles and cook, stirring often, until tender. Drain noodles and return to pot. Add all but 1 teaspoon miso-butter mixture, stirring to coat, then adjust consistency with up to ¼ cup hot water as needed. Season with salt and pepper to taste, cover to keep warm, and set aside until ready to serve.

2. Heat 2 teaspoons vegetable oil in 12-inch nonstick skillet over medium-high heat until shimmering. Add eggplant and cook, stirring occasionally, until tender and deeply browned, 8 to 10 minutes. Combine eggplant in bowl with remaining 1 teaspoon miso-butter mixture and toss to coat; cover with aluminum foil and set aside until ready to serve.

3. Heat remaining 1 teaspoon vegetable oil in now-empty skillet over medium-high heat until shimmering. Add pork and cook, breaking up meat with wooden spoon, until browned and crispy in spots, about 4 minutes. Add soy sauce, garlic, ginger, sesame oil, and sliced scallions whites and cook until fragrant, about 30 seconds.

4. Divide noodles among individual serving bowls. Top with eggplant and pork and sprinkle with remaining sliced scallion greens. Serve.

■ **CUSTOMIZE IT**

Kick it up a notch	Add Quick Pickled Carrot Ribbons (page 217) and/or store-bought pickled ginger.
Instead of soba noodles	Substitute your favorite dried noodle or fresh Chinese noodles.
Instead of eggplant	Try zucchini, snap peas, or snow peas, cooked until spotty brown.
Instead of pork	Substitute ground chicken.

Peanut Soba Noodle Bowl

Serves 2 | **Calories per Serving: 6600**

Why This Recipe Works We love the combination of earthy buckwheat soba noodles and rich peanut sauce as a base for a bowl with ample opportunity to customize toppings. The peanut sauce comes together easily in a blender and adds well-balanced sweet-salty-spicy flavors. We rinsed the noodles after cooking to cool them down and remove extra starch (which would have overly thickened the sauce) before tossing them in our creamy peanut sauce to create a richly flavored noodle base. For easy toppings that added both texture and color, we turned to vibrant shredded red cabbage for crunch, although you could easily try out different combinations of vegetables with this base. Shredded chicken added a hefty dose of protein. The herbaceous notes of fresh cilantro leaves paired well with the ginger, sesame, and peanut flavors of the sauce. We finished our simple but satisfying noodle bowl with a sprinkle of chopped roasted peanuts to complement the sauce, and lime wedges for a squeeze of acidity. You can use store-bought coleslaw mix in place of the red cabbage. Any shredded cooked chicken would work in this bowl; see page 194 for two recipes.

6 ounces soba noodles	2 tablespoons fresh cilantro leaves
¼ cup Peanut-Sesame Sauce (page 222)	2 tablespoons chopped dry-roasted
2 cups shredded cooked chicken	peanuts
½ cup shredded red cabbage	Lime wedges

Bring 2 quarts water to boil in large saucepan. Add noodles and cook, stirring often, until tender. Drain noodles and rinse thoroughly with cold water, shaking to remove excess water. Toss noodles with sauce, adjust consistency with up to ¼ cup hot water as needed, and season with salt and pepper to taste. Divide among individual serving bowls then top with chicken, cabbage, cilantro, and peanuts. Serve with lime wedges.

■ CUSTOMIZE IT

Make it vegan	Substitute edamame or Pan-Seared Tofu (page 198) for the chicken.
For extra crunch	Sliced radishes, cucumbers, bean sprouts, or shredded carrots would all be good here.
Kick it up a notch	Mint, chives, or scallions would bring even more layers of flavor.
Instead of peanuts	Sprinkle with toasted sesame seeds.
Instead of soba noodles	Substitute your favorite dried noodle or fresh Chinese noodles.

Indian-Spiced Chicken Zoodle Bowl

Serves 2 | Calories per Serving: 340

Why This Recipe Works For a fast and flavorful weeknight bowl, we paired adaptable, quick-cooking zucchini noodles with bold Indian flavors that transformed our zoodles from mild to magnificent. Starting with the Indian spice mixture garam masala (which contains a range of spices like cumin, coriander, cinnamon, and black pepper) gave us exciting flavor without needing to use every spice in our pantry. Garlic and ginger added balanced flavor to our chicken before cooking. A few dollops of cilantro-mint yogurt sauce added cooling freshness and tang, and diced mango tossed with more cilantro lent a touch of sweetness. Cooking the zoodles in two batches ensured that the delicate "noodles" didn't overcook and turn mushy. You will need 1 pound of zucchini to get 12 ounces of noodles; we prefer to make our own using a spiralizer (see page 193), but in a pinch you can use store-bought. Cook the zucchini to your desired level of doneness but be careful not to overcook.

½ mango, peeled and cut into ¼-inch pieces
1 tablespoon chopped fresh cilantro
1 teaspoon lemon juice
2 garlic cloves, minced
1 teaspoon grated fresh ginger
4 teaspoons vegetable oil, divided
2 teaspoons garam masala, divided

¼ teaspoon table salt, divided
¼ teaspoon pepper, divided
8 ounces boneless, skinless chicken breasts, trimmed and cut into ½-inch pieces
12 ounces zucchini noodles, cut into 6-inch lengths, divided
½ cup Herb-Yogurt Sauce (page 226)

1. Combine mango, cilantro, and lemon juice in bowl; season with salt and pepper to taste and set aside until ready to serve. Whisk garlic, ginger, 1 teaspoon oil, 1 teaspoon garam masala, ⅛ teaspoon salt, and ⅛ teaspoon pepper together in medium bowl, then add chicken and toss to coat.

2. Heat 1 teaspoon oil in 12-inch nonstick skillet over medium-high heat until shimmering. Add chicken and cook until browned on all sides, 4 to 6 minutes. Transfer to clean bowl, cover with aluminum foil to keep warm, and set aside until ready to serve.

3. Heat 1 teaspoon oil in now-empty skillet over medium-high heat until shimmering. Add ½ teaspoon garam masala, pinch salt, pinch pepper, and half of zucchini noodles and cook, tossing frequently, until crisp-tender, about 1 minute. Transfer to individual serving bowl and repeat with remaining 1 teaspoon oil, remaining ½ teaspoon garam masala, remaining pinch salt, remaining pinch pepper, and remaining zucchini noodles. Top zucchini noodles with chicken, mango mixture, and sauce. Serve.

■ **CUSTOMIZE IT**

For extra crunch	Top with chopped toasted cashews.
Kick it up a notch	Add a minced Fresno or Thai chile to the diced mango.
Instead of mango	Chopped pineapple would also work; you'll need about 1 cup.
Simplify the sauce	Use plain yogurt in place of the Herb-Yogurt Sauce.

Shrimp Saganaki Zoodle Bowl

Serves 2　|　Calories per Serving: 340

Why This Recipe Works　Shrimp saganaki is a classic Greek dish of shrimp in a rich and zesty tomato sauce sprinkled with herbs and feta cheese. We knew this quick-cooking, flavorful yet light dish would work well as a bowl paired with (even quicker-cooking) zucchini noodles. To put a fresh spin on the tomato sauce that wouldn't weigh down our delicate zoodles, we sautéed cherry tomatoes until they were bursting with sweet juice and added artichoke hearts (for meatiness), fresh dill, and lemon zest to create a chunky topping. Seasoned simply with salt and pepper, the zucchini noodles were an updated pairing for the bold tomato-artichoke sauce and lemony sautéed shrimp. Crumbled feta and chopped kalamata olives brought bites of pleasant brininess. You will need 1 pound of zucchini to get 12 ounces of noodles; we prefer to make our own using a spiralizer (see page 193), but in a pinch you can use store-bought. Cook the zucchini to your desired level of doneness but be careful not to overcook. After preparing the sautéed shrimp, you can reuse the skillet for the sauce and zoodles.

2 tablespoons extra-virgin olive oil, divided
1 shallot, minced
1 garlic clove, minced
6 ounces cherry tomatoes, halved
1 cup jarred whole artichoke hearts packed in water, rinsed, patted dry, and halved
½ teaspoon grated lemon zest, plus lemon wedges for serving

¼ teaspoon table salt, divided
¼ teaspoon pepper, divided
1 tablespoon chopped fresh dill
12 ounces zucchini noodles, cut into 6-inch lengths, divided
¾ cup Sautéed Lemony Shrimp (page 197), warmed
1 ounce feta cheese, crumbled (¼ cup)
2 tablespoons pitted kalamata olives, chopped

1. Heat 1 teaspoon oil in 12-inch nonstick skillet over medium heat until shimmering. Add shallot and garlic and cook until fragrant, about 30 seconds. Stir in tomatoes, artichoke hearts, lemon zest, ⅛ teaspoon salt, and ⅛ teaspoon pepper and cook, stirring frequently, until tomatoes have softened, 3 to 5 minutes. Transfer to bowl and stir in dill and 1 tablespoon oil. Cover with aluminum foil to keep warm and set aside until ready to serve.

2. Wipe out skillet with paper towels. Heat 1 teaspoon oil in now-empty skillet over medium-high heat until shimmering. Add half of zucchini noodles, pinch salt, and pinch pepper and cook, tossing frequently, until crisp-tender, about 1 minute. Transfer to individual serving bowl and repeat with remaining 1 teaspoon oil, remaining zucchini noodles, remaining pinch salt, and remaining pinch pepper. Top zucchini noodles with tomato-artichoke mixture, shrimp, feta, and olives. Serve with lemon wedges.

■ **CUSTOMIZE IT**

Instead of shrimp	Seared Chicken Breasts (page 194) or Oven-Roasted Salmon (page 197) can also be used.
Instead of dill	Try basil or parsley.
Instead of feta	Use halloumi or goat cheese.
Instead of artichokes	Try chopped roasted red peppers (or use both).
For extra crunch	Sprinkle on homemade (page 215) or store-bought croutons.

Mediterranean Carrot Noodle Bowl

Serves 2 | **Calories per Serving: 350**

Why This Recipe Works For a light, refreshing take on a noodle bowl, we decided to forgo starchy noodles in favor of naturally sweet carrot noodles. Pairing them with a spicy harissa vinaigrette and peppery arugula created a boldly flavored bowl with smoky heat and earthy spice. Chopped mint gave contrasting freshness, while jammy bites of dried apricots echoed the carrots' sweetness and provided chewy texture. Topping our jewel-colored bowl with crumbled goat cheese added creaminess and tang that was a perfect contrast to our smoky carrot noodle base. We prefer our homemade harissa in this recipe, but you can substitute store-bought harissa if you wish, though spiciness can vary greatly by brand. You will need 1 pound of carrots to get 12 ounces of noodles; we prefer to make our own using a spiralizer (see page 193), but in a pinch you can use store-bought. For the best noodles, use carrots that are at least ¾ inch wide at the thinnest end and 1½ inches wide at the thickest end.

2 tablespoons Harissa (page 222)	12 ounces carrot noodles, cut into 6-inch lengths
2 tablespoons lemon juice	2 cups (2 ounces) baby arugula
1 tablespoon water	¼ cup chopped fresh mint, divided
2 teaspoons honey	2 ounces goat cheese, crumbled (½ cup)
⅛ teaspoon table salt	¼ cup dried apricots, sliced thin
⅛ teaspoon pepper	

1. Whisk harissa, lemon juice, water, honey, salt, and pepper together in large bowl. Measure out and reserve 1 tablespoon vinaigrette for serving.

2. Add carrot noodles, arugula, and 3 tablespoons mint to bowl with vinaigrette and toss to coat; season with salt and pepper to taste. Divide among individual serving bowls then top with goat cheese and apricots and sprinkle with remaining 1 tablespoon mint. Drizzle with reserved vinaigrette. Serve.

■ CUSTOMIZE IT

Kick it up a notch	Add pistachios, walnuts, Crispy Chickpeas (page 212), or Savory Seed Brittle (page 211). Use multicolored carrots or a mixture of beet and carrot noodles for extra color.
Instead of apricots	Golden raisins or dried figs would also work.

Lemony Linguine Bowl

Serves 2 | Calories per Serving: 530

Why This Recipe Works Lemony pasta bowls are a refreshing change from the typical red sauce, and to take the simple components of this dish to the next level we packed in lemon flavor and incorporated a few easy, but surprisingly satisfying, toppings. We started with a crunchy bread-crumb topping that requires nothing more than a bowl and a microwave. After a few minutes of stirring we ended up with perfectly golden-brown bread crumbs, no skillet required. For the sauce, we started by mixing umami-packed Parmesan cheese with garlic, lemon juice, and lemon zest. We found that the addition of zest really improved the lemon punch without making the sauce too acidic. Once the pasta was cooked, we reserved some of the cooking water to help the lemon mixture cling to the noodles and also threw in a handful of raw spinach until it slowly wilted from the heat of the pasta. A little basil on top completed this satisfying, speedy, and simple bowl.

- 2 tablespoons panko bread crumbs
- 2 tablespoons plus 2 teaspoons extra-virgin olive oil, divided
- ¼ cup grated Parmesan cheese, plus extra for serving
- 1 teaspoon grated lemon zest plus 2 tablespoons juice
- 1 garlic clove, minced
- ⅛ teaspoon table salt, plus salt for cooking pasta
- ¼ teaspoon pepper
- 6 ounces linguine
- 3 ounces (3 cups) baby spinach
- 2 tablespoons chopped fresh basil

1. Toss panko with 2 teaspoons oil in bowl until evenly coated. Microwave, stirring frequently, until light golden brown, 1 to 3 minutes; set aside to cool.

2. Whisk Parmesan, remaining 2 tablespoons oil, lemon zest and juice, garlic, ⅛ teaspoon salt, and pepper together in small bowl; set aside.

3. Bring 2 quarts water to boil in large saucepan. Add pasta and 1 tablespoon salt and cook, stirring often, until tender. Reserve ¼ cup cooking water then drain pasta and return it to pot. Stir in Parmesan mixture and spinach, tossing until spinach is slightly wilted and pasta is well coated, about 1 minute. Adjust consistency with reserved cooking water as needed and season with salt and pepper to taste. Divide among individual serving bowls then sprinkle with bread crumbs and basil. Serve, passing extra Parmesan separately.

■ **CUSTOMIZE IT**

Kick it up a notch	Add 1 Fried Egg (page 199) to each bowl. Serve with lemon wedges.
Instead of panko	Use Frico Crumble (page 214) or use store-bought Parmesan crisps and skip step 1.

Spinach Pesto Noodle Bowl

Serves 2 | Calories per Serving: 500

Why This Recipe Works Basil pesto often steals the spotlight, but for a supernutritious, not-too-oily pesto that can take on fresh flavors in a bowl, we love using spinach instead of basil. Spinach pesto couldn't be simpler to make; sauté some onion and garlic, followed by a hefty amount of spinach, then process in a food processor with Parmesan, lemon juice, and a little pasta water. Once we stirred the pesto into the pasta, we knew we had a winner, but it was missing something. Earthy, nutty artichoke hearts rounded out the flavors and bulked up the dish. We then topped the pasta with sautéed cherry tomatoes, which lent brightness, while a sprinkle of basil added pleasant freshness. For a spicier dish, add more pepper flakes.

1 tablespoon extra-virgin olive oil
1 small onion, chopped fine
1 garlic clove, minced
  Pinch red pepper flakes
5 ounces (5 cups) baby spinach
  Table salt
6 ounces spaghetti
¼ cup grated Parmesan cheese

1 teaspoon lemon juice
1 cup drained jarred whole baby artichoke hearts packed in water, quartered
1 cup Sautéed Cherry Tomatoes (page 205), warmed
1 tablespoon chopped fresh basil

1. Heat oil in 12-inch nonstick skillet over medium heat until shimmering. Add onion and cook until softened and lightly browned, 5 to 7 minutes. Stir in garlic and pepper flakes and cook until fragrant, about 30 seconds. Add spinach, one handful at a time, and ½ teaspoon salt and cook until wilted, about 2 minutes.

2. Meanwhile, bring 2 quarts water to boil in large saucepan. Add pasta and 1 tablespoon salt and cook, stirring often, until tender. Reserve ½ cup cooking water, then drain pasta and return it to pot.

3. Transfer spinach mixture to food processor along with Parmesan, lemon juice, and ¼ cup reserved cooking water. Process until smooth, about 1 minute, scraping down sides of bowl as needed. Add spinach puree and artichokes to pot with pasta and stir to coat. Adjust consistency of sauce with remaining ¼ cup reserved cooking water as needed and season with salt and pepper to taste. Divide among individual serving bowls then top with tomatoes and sprinkle with basil. Serve.

■ CUSTOMIZE IT

Make it creamy	Dollop with ricotta cheese before serving.
For extra crunch	Add Garlic Chips (page 214) and/or Crispy Shallots (page 212).

Creamy Corn Bucatini Bowl

Serves 2　│　Calories per Serving: 590

Why This Recipe Works　With just seven ingredients, this creamy pasta bowl delivers on fresh, summery flavor thanks to a rich sauce made using corn kernels and milk. To start, we took kernels off the cob, reserving some to add crunchy contrast and using the rest to make our sauce. After quickly simmering the corn in milk, we pureed it all in a blender and then pushed our sauce through a fine-mesh strainer for a smooth consistency. Next, we added partially cooked bucatini and some pasta water to the corn sauce and cooked it together until the pasta was tender and the sauce had thickened to a silken texture. We topped the pasta with creamy dollops of ricotta, pieces of torn basil, and our remaining fresh corn. You will need about 3 ears of fresh corn to get 2¼ cups kernels. Frozen corn that is thawed may be substituted for fresh corn; cook reserved ¼ cup corn in microwave until steaming and tender, 30 to 60 seconds. If you can't find bucatini, you can use spaghetti, though you should reduce the step 2 cooking time to 4 minutes.

2¼ cups fresh or thawed frozen corn kernels, divided

⅔ cup whole milk

6 ounces bucatini

¼ teaspoon table salt, plus salt for cooking pasta

¼ teaspoon red pepper flakes

3 ounces (⅓ cup) whole-milk ricotta cheese

2 tablespoons chopped fresh basil

1. Bring 2 cups corn and milk to simmer in 12-inch skillet over medium heat. Carefully transfer corn and milk to blender and let cool slightly, about 5 minutes. Process until smooth, about 3 minutes, scraping down sides of blender jar as needed. Strain corn mixture through fine-mesh strainer into now-empty skillet, pressing on solids to extract as much liquid as possible.

2. Meanwhile, bring 2 quarts water to boil in large saucepan. Add pasta and 1 tablespoon salt and cook, stirring often, until pasta is flexible but still firm, about 5 minutes. Reserve ¾ cup cooking water, then drain pasta.

3. Stir pasta, ½ cup reserved cooking water, salt, and pepper flakes into corn mixture in skillet. Cook over medium heat, stirring constantly, until pasta is tender and well coated, 3 to 5 minutes. Adjust consistency with remaining reserved cooking water as needed and season with salt and pepper to taste. Divide among individual serving bowls, then dollop with ricotta and sprinkle with basil and remaining ¼ cup corn. Serve.

■ **CUSTOMIZE IT**

For extra crunch　│　Add Frico Crumble (page 214) or crisped prosciutto or bacon.

Kick it up a notch　│　Add Sautéed Cherry Tomatoes (page 205).

Roasted Cauliflower and Brown Butter Noodle Bowl

Serves 2 | Calories per Serving: 690

Why This Recipe Works The ultimate pantry-friendly pasta bowl, this incredibly simple combination pairs warm pasta, make-ahead cauliflower, and briny capers with a brown butter sauce. Brown butter—simply cooking melted butter until the milk proteins turn golden brown—makes for a light but satisfying sauce that adds nutty and caramelized flavors. Hearty roasted cauliflower, with its natural sweetness and nuttiness, can easily be made in advance, but you could also try out other vegetables. Roasting the cauliflower in wedges allows for maximum browning (and flavor development), and covering it during the first part of roasting ensures that it doesn't dry out. For brightness, we added a healthy dose of minced capers and some lemon juice to the sauce and then served the bowls with lemon wedges for adding extra zing. Tossing in whole fresh parsley leaves brought color, texture, and fresh flavor to complete our bowls.

6 ounces spaghetti	1½ teaspoons lemon juice, plus lemon
Table salt for cooking pasta	wedges for serving
4 tablespoons unsalted butter	½ cup fresh parsley leaves, divided
2 tablespoon capers, rinsed and minced	1 recipe Roasted Cauliflower
	(page 205), warmed

1. Bring 2 quarts water to boil in large saucepan. Add pasta and 1 tablespoon salt and cook, stirring often, until tender. Reserve ¼ cup cooking water, then drain pasta and return it to pot.

2. Melt butter in 12-inch skillet over medium heat. Continue to cook, stirring frequently until butter is dark golden brown and has nutty aroma, 1 to 3 minutes longer. Off heat, stir in capers and lemon juice. Add pasta and ⅓ cup parsley and toss to coat, adding reserved cooking water to adjust consistency as needed; season with salt and pepper to taste. Divide among individual serving bowls, then top with cauliflower and remaining parsley. Serve with lemon wedges.

■ **CUSTOMIZE IT**

For extra crunch	Add toasted pine nuts, hazelnuts, or Frico Crumble (page 214).
Instead of cauliflower	Use Roasted Butternut Squash (page 203) or Sautéed Mushrooms with Shallots and Thyme (page 207).
Instead of parsley	Add 1 teaspoon minced sage to skillet with capers in step 2.

Tagliatelle alla Norma Bowl

Serves 2 | **Calories per Serving: 550**

Why This Recipe Works Pasta *alla norma* makes for a hearty, vegetable-filled pasta bowl with its lively combination of tender eggplant, robust tomato sauce, al dente pasta, and salty, milky ricotta salata. For our spin on the classic, we sautéed the eggplant separate from the sauce to create flavorful browning. A can of whole peeled tomatoes, processed in a food processor, was the perfect consistency and flavor to start off our sauce, giving us a brighter, fresher sauce than crushed tomatoes would. We used simple aromatics, onion and garlic, but also added in anchovy for savoriness and red pepper flakes for some spice. A little sugar helped balance the flavors. To finish off our bowl, ricotta salata added bite, and some fresh basil added herby depth.

1 (14.5-ounce) can whole peeled tomatoes

2 tablespoons extra-virgin olive oil, divided

8 ounces eggplant, cut into ½-inch pieces

⅛ teaspoon table salt, plus salt for cooking pasta

⅛ teaspoon pepper

1 garlic clove, minced

1 anchovy fillet, rinsed, patted dry, and minced

⅛ teaspoon red pepper flakes

1 teaspoon sugar

6 ounces tagliatelle

3 tablespoons chopped fresh basil, divided

1 ounce ricotta salata cheese, shredded (¼ cup)

1. Process tomatoes and their juice in food processor until smooth, about 30 seconds; set aside. Heat 1 tablespoon oil in 12-inch nonstick skillet over medium-high heat until just smoking. Add eggplant, salt, and pepper and cook, stirring occasionally, until eggplant is tender and deeply browned, 8 to 10 minutes. Transfer to bowl, cover with aluminum foil to keep warm, and set aside until ready to serve.

2. Add remaining 1 tablespoon oil, garlic, anchovy, and pepper flakes to now-empty skillet and cook over medium heat until fragrant, about 30 seconds. Stir in processed tomatoes, ¼ cup water, and sugar, bring to simmer, and cook over medium-low heat until slightly thickened, 12 to 15 minutes.

3. Meanwhile, bring 2 quarts water to boil in large saucepan. Add pasta and 1 tablespoon salt and cook, stirring often, until al dente. Reserve ¼ cup cooking water, then drain pasta and return it to pot. Add tomato mixture and 1 tablespoon basil and toss to combine, adjusting consistency with reserved cooking water as needed; season with salt and pepper to taste. Divide among individual serving bowls, then top with eggplant and ricotta salata and sprinkle with remaining 2 tablespoons basil. Serve.

■ CUSTOMIZE IT

For extra crunch	Sprinkle with toasted pine nuts or Garlic Chips (page 214).
For extra brininess	Add chopped kalamata olives.
Instead of ricotta salata	Try Parmesan cheese or Pecorino Romano cheese.

soup
bowls

Ramen Zoodle Bowl

Curried Coconut Shrimp Soup

Serves 2 | **Calories per Serving: 510**

Why This Recipe Works Replete with bright vegetables and juicy shrimp, this aromatic Thai-style soup is perfectly sized to serve two and comes together in record time. To infuse our soup with flavor quickly, we bloomed store-bought Thai green curry paste in oil before adding a combination of chicken broth and coconut milk for a rich, fragrant base, which we then seasoned with lime juice and fish sauce for sour-salty flavor. Sweet potatoes, which cooked in the broth in just 10 minutes, added substance as well as a balancing sweetness. Lightly sautéed sweet shrimp made for the perfect addition, and a fast topping of sliced snow peas and fresh cilantro lent bright, crunchy texture. The sweet potatoes become very tender in this dish; be sure to stir the soup gently to prevent them from breaking up too much.

1 teaspoon vegetable oil
1 tablespoon Thai green curry paste
½ teaspoon red pepper flakes
2 cups chicken or vegetable broth, plus extra as needed
¾ cup canned coconut milk
8 ounces sweet potatoes, peeled and cut into ½-inch pieces
1 tablespoon lime juice
2 teaspoons fish sauce
1 recipe Sautéed Shrimp (page 197)
2 ounces snow peas, strings removed and sliced thin lengthwise
¼ cup fresh cilantro leaves

1. Heat oil in large saucepan over medium-high heat until shimmering. Add curry paste and pepper flakes and cook until fragrant, about 30 seconds. Stir in broth, coconut milk, and potatoes, scraping up any browned bits. Bring to simmer, then reduce heat to low, cover, and cook until potatoes are tender, 10 to 12 minutes. Off heat, stir in lime juice and fish sauce and season with salt and pepper to taste.

2. Divide soup among individual serving bowls then top with shrimp, snow peas, and cilantro. Serve.

■ CUSTOMIZE IT

Kick it up a notch | Tender sautéed bok choy would bulk up the soup with even more vegetables.

Instead of shrimp | Seared scallops, flaky white fish like cod or halibut, or even cooked chicken or tofu would all work.

Vietnamese Beef Pho

Serves 2 | **Calories per Serving: 520**

Why This Recipe Works Assembled just before serving and customized at the table with plentiful garnishes, pho is the pinnacle of bowl food. While the fragrant broth traditionally simmers for hours, our dead-simple approach infuses aromatic flavor into store-bought beef broth in just 30 minutes using onion, ginger, cinnamon, star anise, and cloves. Instead of painstakingly slicing steak, which cooks at the last second in the hot broth, store-bought shaved steak (often used for steak sandwiches) stood in perfectly. If you can't find it, freeze 8 ounces trimmed strip steak until very firm and slice ⅛ inch thick against the grain. The strained broth can be refrigerated for up to 2 days; bring it to a boil before serving.

1 small onion, quartered through
 root end, divided
3 cups beef broth
1 tablespoon fish sauce, plus
 extra for serving
1 (1-inch) piece ginger, sliced
 into thin rounds
1 cinnamon stick
2 teaspoons sugar
2 star anise pods
4 whole cloves
6 ounces (¼-inch-wide) rice noodles
8 ounces shaved steak
1 ounce (½ cup) bean sprouts
⅓ cup fresh cilantro leaves
 Lime wedges

1. Slice 1 onion quarter as thin as possible; set aside until ready to serve. Bring remaining 3 onion quarters, broth, 1 cup water, fish sauce, ginger, cinnamon, sugar, star anise, and cloves to boil in large saucepan, then reduce heat to medium-low and simmer for 30 minutes. While broth simmers, pour 2 quarts boiling water over noodles in bowl and stir to separate. Let noodles soak until soft and pliable but not fully tender, stirring once halfway through soaking, 8 to 10 minutes. Drain noodles and rinse with cold water until water runs clear, shaking to remove excess water.

2. Strain broth through fine-mesh strainer into 4-cup liquid measuring cup, adding water as needed to equal 3 cups. Discard solids. Combine noodles and broth in now-empty saucepan, return to boil, and cook until noodles are tender, about 1 minute. Season with salt and pepper to taste.

3. Divide hot broth and noodles among individual serving bowls then stir in thinly sliced onion and steak. Top with sprouts and cilantro. Serve immediately, passing lime wedges and extra fish sauce separately.

■ CUSTOMIZE IT

Kick it up a notch	An abundance of herbs is traditional in pho; if you can find it, add Thai basil for big flavor. Drizzle on sriracha or hoisin.
Instead of beef	Sautéed Shrimp (page 197) or cubed tofu work.

Mexican Street-Corn Chowder

Serves 2 | Calories per Serving: 420

Why This Recipe Works Sweet corn, tangy lime, spicy chili powder, and fresh cilantro combine in this soup inspired by the popular Mexican street food, ensuring that each spoonful hits all the taste buds. To make the soup even more interesting, we prepared two easy toppings, first sautéing poblano chiles for vegetal depth, and then cooking up Mexican chorizo until it turned deliciously crispy and rendered some flavorful fat, which we used to toast our corn. After adding chicken broth and aromatics to the corn, we pureed most of it until creamy, leaving some corn kernels whole for a pleasant chunky texture. A final sprinkling of cilantro added bright freshness.

 1 tablespoon vegetable oil, divided
 2 poblano chiles, stemmed, seeded, and sliced thin
 4 garlic cloves, minced, divided
 1¼ teaspoons chili powder, divided
 2 ounces Mexican-style chorizo sausage, casings removed

 4 ears corn, kernels cut from cobs (3½ cups)
 ⅛ teaspoon table salt
 1½ cups chicken broth
 ¼ cup chopped fresh cilantro
 Lime wedges for serving

1. Heat 1 teaspoon oil in large saucepan over medium heat until shimmering. Add poblanos and cook until just tender, 3 to 5 minutes. Stir in one-fourth of garlic and ¼ teaspoon chili powder and cook until fragrant. Transfer to bowl, cover with aluminum foil, and set aside until ready to serve. In now-empty saucepan, heat remaining 2 teaspoons oil over medium heat until shimmering. Add chorizo and cook until browned, about 3 minutes, breaking up meat with wooden spoon. Using slotted spoon, transfer chorizo to second bowl, covering with foil to keep warm.

2. Pour off all but 1 teaspoon fat from saucepan. (If necessary, add oil to equal 1 teaspoon.) Add corn to fat left in pot and cook over medium heat, stirring occasionally and scraping up any browned bits, until corn is lightly browned, about 5 minutes. Stir in remaining garlic, ¾ teaspoon chili powder, and salt and cook until fragrant, about 30 seconds. Stir in chicken broth, scraping up any browned bits, and bring to simmer. Cook until corn is tender, about 2 minutes.

3. Process 2 cups soup in blender until very smooth, about 1 minute. Stir pureed soup into remaining soup in saucepan, adjusting consistency with hot water as needed, and season with salt and pepper to taste. Divide soup among individual serving bowls then top with poblanos, chorizo, cilantro, and remaining ¼ teaspoon chili powder. Serve with lime wedges.

▦ CUSTOMIZE IT

Kick it up a notch	For a creamy topping and even more brightness, mix a quick sauce of sour cream and lime juice; or add a dollop of Chipotle-Yogurt Sauce (page 226) for extra spice.
Instead of fresh corn	If fresh corn isn't in season, frozen corn can be used instead.
Instead of Mexican chorizo	Use dried Spanish chorizo or andouille sausage, cut into pieces.

Green Pork Posole Bowl

Serves 2 | Calories per Serving: 550

Why This Recipe Works For an everyday bowl inspired by Mexican green posole, a typically long-simmered pork and hominy stew, we exchanged slow-cooking pork shoulder for ground pork and used two types of chile peppers—poblano and jalapeño—for complex spiciness. Tomatillos form the classic base for a green posole; to achieve the perfect chunky consistency, we mashed canned tomatillos and simmered them with our other ingredients until the stew thickened slightly and the flavors melded. Toppings of *queso fresco* and chopped tomato gave the posole bright, fresh flavor. Both white hominy and yellow hominy will work in this stew; however, we prefer the deeper flavor of white hominy here. To make this dish spicier, include the seeds from the chiles.

1 teaspoon vegetable oil
8 ounces ground pork
1 small onion, chopped fine
1 poblano chile, stemmed, seeded, and chopped
1 jalapeño chile, stemmed, seeded, and minced
1 (12-ounce) can tomatillos, drained
2 garlic cloves, minced

½ teaspoon ground cumin
¼ teaspoon cayenne pepper
2 cups chicken broth
1 (15-ounce) can white hominy, rinsed
1 tomato, cored and cut into ½-inch pieces
1 ounce queso fresco, crumbled (¼ cup)

1. Heat oil in large saucepan over medium heat until shimmering. Add pork, onion, poblano, and jalapeño and cook, breaking up meat with wooden spoon, until no longer pink, about 5 minutes. Meanwhile, coarsely mash tomatillos with potato masher in bowl; set aside.

2. Stir garlic, cumin, and cayenne into pork mixture in saucepan and cook until fragrant, about 1 minute. Stir in tomatillos, broth, and hominy, scraping up any browned bits with wooden spoon. Bring to simmer and cook, stirring occasionally, until stew is slightly thickened, about 15 minutes. Season with salt and pepper to taste.

3. Divide soup among individual serving bowls then top with tomato and queso fresco. Serve.

■ CUSTOMIZE IT

Kick it up a notch	For a fun and absolutely appropriate garnish (it's corn after all!), a handful of popcorn gives the stew a pleasant crunch. For even more herbal freshness, add a sprinkling of cilantro leaves.
Instead of queso fresco	Feta makes for a deliciously tangy substitution.
Instead of canned tomatillos	You can certainly use fresh tomatillos if they are available; just be sure to chop them before mashing.

Gazpacho Bowl

Serves 4 | Calories per Serving: 80

Why This Recipe Works Bright gazpacho with a bounty of fresh vegetables makes for a perfect summery, on-the-go meal since it's typically served cold. But many recipes produce bland, thin soups that feel like an insubstantial meal. We wanted a foolproof, quick, simple recipe for a gazpacho with distinct vegetable chunks in a bold and bracing tomato broth that had enough heft to hold a variety of toppings. Chopping our vegetables in a food processor saved us from the tedious task of chopping by hand and ensured that our summery soup would have similar-size chunks of vegetables. Extra tomato juice rounded out our broth, and with some salt and pepper, vinegar, shallot, and garlic we had a soup with deep, bold flavor. For kick, a small amount of hot sauce went a long way to enliven our soup. With our substantial gazpacho complete, we were free to pile on toppings; see the ideas below. White wine vinegar can be substituted for the sherry vinegar. Once assembled, the soup can be refrigerated for up to 1 day; season with additional salt and pepper before serving.

1 red bell pepper, stemmed, seeded, and chopped coarse

1 cucumber, peeled, halved lengthwise, seeded, and chopped coarse

1 pound tomatoes, cored and quartered

2½ cups tomato juice

1 large shallot, minced

2 tablespoons sherry vinegar, plus extra as needed

1 garlic clove, minced

1 teaspoon table salt

½ teaspoon pepper

½ teaspoon hot sauce

1. Pulse bell pepper and cucumber in food processor to ¼- to ½-inch pieces, about 6 pulses; transfer to large bowl. Repeat with tomatoes.

2. Stir in tomato juice, shallot, vinegar, garlic, salt, pepper, and hot sauce until thoroughly combined. Season with additional salt, pepper, and vinegar to taste. Divide among individual serving bowls. Serve.

■ **CUSTOMIZE IT**

Add crunch	Add homemade Croutons (page 215) or store-bought croutons.
Make it heartier	Add chopped Easy-Peel Hard-Cooked Eggs (page 199).
Kick it up a notch	Chopped olives and avocado would add savory bite and creamy texture.

Turkey Chili Bowl

Serves 2 | Calories per Serving: 450

Why This Recipe Works Few dishes are more comforting—or more versatile—than chili, but we don't always want to simmer a giant pot of it. For a spontaneous chili for two, we took a lean, but no less flavorful, approach, using ground turkey instead of beef. To protect it from drying out, we tossed it with a mixture of water and baking soda, which helped the turkey hold on to its moisture. For the perfect thick, hearty consistency, we mashed a portion of the beans. Our ultraquick homemade salsa and a dollop of sour cream added bright, fresh flavor and tanginess. Be sure to use ground turkey, not ground turkey breast (also labeled 99 percent fat-free), in this recipe.

8 ounces ground turkey
2 teaspoons water
⅛ teaspoon baking soda
1 tablespoon vegetable oil
2 tablespoons chili powder
4 garlic cloves, minced

1 (15-ounce) can pinto beans, rinsed
1 cup chicken broth
½ cup One-Minute Tomato Salsa (page 227)
¼ cup sour cream
   Lime wedges

1. Toss turkey, water, and baking soda in bowl until thoroughly combined. Cover with plastic wrap and refrigerate for 15 minutes.

2. Heat oil in large saucepan over medium heat until shimmering. Add turkey mixture and cook, breaking up meat with wooden spoon, until no pink remains, about 4 minutes. Stir in chili powder and garlic and cook until fragrant, about 30 seconds. Stir in beans and broth and bring to simmer. Reduce heat to low and cook until chili is slightly thickened, about 10 minutes.

3. Remove pot from heat and, using potato masher, gently mash half of beans in pot. Stir to recombine and season with salt and pepper to taste. Divide chili among individual serving bowls, then top with salsa and sour cream. Serve with lime wedges.

■ CUSTOMIZE IT

Add crunch	Crumbled sweet potato chips make a fun topping that complements the turkey's flavor; tortilla chips work, too.
Kick it up a notch	Add traditional chili toppings of lettuce, jalapeños, or cheese.
Instead of turkey	Ground chicken, 85% lean ground beef, or ground pork would work.
Instead of pinto beans	Black beans would make for a tasty alternative.
Simplify the chili	Use your favorite store-bought salsa.

Caldo Verde Bowl

Serves 6 to 8 │ **Calories per Serving: 370**

Why This Recipe Works One of the simplest of soups, Portuguese caldo verde combines tender potatoes and slightly sweet collard greens with smoked sausage. The sausage (we used Spanish chorizo) is usually simmered with the soup but we loved the contrast it provided when cooked until browned and sprinkled on as a topping; we used the chorizo's rendered fat to sauté our broth's aromatics. Pureeing a portion of the soup to a luxuriously creamy consistency ensured the perfect balance of rich broth and hearty potato pieces.

3 tablespoons plus 1 teaspoon extra-virgin olive oil, divided

12 ounces Spanish-style chorizo sausage, cut into 1/2-inch pieces

1 onion, chopped fine

4 garlic cloves, minced

1 1/4 teaspoons table salt

1/4 teaspoon red pepper flakes

2 pounds Yukon Gold potatoes, peeled and cut into 3/4-inch pieces

4 cups chicken broth

4 cups water

1 pound collard greens, stemmed and cut into 1-inch pieces

2 teaspoons white wine vinegar

1. Heat 1 teaspoon oil in Dutch oven over medium-high heat until shimmering. Add chorizo and cook, stirring occasionally, until lightly browned, 3 to 5 minutes. Using slotted spoon, transfer chorizo to bowl; set aside until ready to serve.

2. Pour off all but 1 tablespoon fat from pot. (If necessary, add oil to equal 1 tablespoon.) Add onion, garlic, salt, and pepper flakes to fat in pot and cook over medium heat, stirring frequently, until onion is translucent, 2 to 3 minutes. Stir in potatoes, broth, and water and bring to boil. Reduce heat to medium-low and simmer until potatoes are just tender, 8 to 10 minutes.

3. Transfer 3/4 cup solids and 3/4 cup broth to blender. Add collard greens to soup left in pot and simmer until greens are tender, 18 to 20 minutes.

4. Add remaining 3 tablespoons oil to soup in blender and process until very smooth, about 1 minute. Off heat, stir pureed soup mixture and vinegar into remaining soup in pot then season with salt and pepper to taste. Divide soup among individual serving bowls then top with chorizo. Serve.

■ **CUSTOMIZE IT**

Kick it up a notch	For bold, herbal flavor, drizzle on Chimichurri Sauce (page 223).
Instead of Spanish chorizo	Mexican chorizo, casings removed and crumbled, could be used instead of Spanish chorizo.
Instead of collards	Kale's hearty texture works as a replacement for the collard greens.

Creamy Butternut Squash Soup with Apples and Pork

Serves 2 | Calories per Serving: 390

Why This Recipe Works Butternut squash soup makes for a rich, creamy soup on its own but can also take on an array of hearty toppings. To simplify the cooking process, we parcooked large chunks of squash in the microwave and let them drain while focusing our attention on cooking a crispy topping of ground pork seasoned with fennel, garlic, and shallot. We then caramelized the squash in the pork's rendered fat to build some flavorful fond before deglazing and pureeing our soup. Fresh apple matchsticks added just the right contrasting crunch and sweetness.

1½ pounds butternut squash, peeled, seeded, and cut into 2-inch pieces (3 cups)

4 ounces ground pork

1 large shallot, minced, divided

1 garlic clove, minced

½ teaspoon ground fennel seeds

¼ teaspoon table salt

1 tablespoon unsalted butter

2 cups chicken broth

1 sprig fresh thyme

½ apple, cored and cut into 2-inch-long matchsticks

1. Microwave squash in covered bowl until paring knife glides easily through flesh, about 10 minutes, stirring once halfway through. Carefully transfer squash to colander set in bowl (squash will be very hot) and let drain for 5 minutes, reserving any liquid.

2. Meanwhile, break up ground pork into small pieces in bowl, then stir in half of shallot, garlic, fennel, and salt until well combined. Melt butter in large saucepan over medium heat. Pinch off ½-inch-size pieces of pork mixture into saucepan and cook, stirring gently, until pork is golden brown, 2 to 4 minutes. Using slotted spoon, transfer pork to bowl.

3. Pour off all but 1 teaspoon fat from saucepan. (If necessary, add oil to equal 1 teaspoon.) Add drained squash and remaining shallot and cook over medium-high heat, stirring occasionally, until squash begins to break down and fond forms on bottom of pot, 5 to 7 minutes. Add reserved squash liquid, broth, and thyme, scraping up any browned bits with wooden spoon. Bring to simmer and cook over medium heat until flavors meld, about 5 minutes.

4. Discard thyme sprig. Process soup in blender until smooth, about 1 minute. Return soup to clean saucepan and bring to brief simmer, adjusting consistency with hot water as needed. Season with salt and pepper to taste. Divide soup among individual serving bowls then top with pork and apple. Serve.

■ CUSTOMIZE IT

Add crunch	Our homemade Savory Seed Brittle (page 211) would make an outstanding topping for this soup.
Kick it up a notch	A drizzle of spicy Zhoug (page 223) would add a punch of bright herbal flavor and heat to complement the soup's autumnal flavors.

Mediterranean Eggplant Soup with Lamb

Serves 2 | Calories per Serving: 350

Why This Recipe Works Eggplant is rich, meaty, and hearty—and when cooked with tomatoes and North African spices yields an unforgettable, tastebud-pleasing soup. To make our soup into a meal, we sautéed ground lamb for a savory topping, then sautéed diced eggplant in the rendered fat to impart char and deep flavor. After reserving some eggplant for a second topping, we simmered the rest with broth, onion, and tomatoes before pureeing. Seasoning both the soup and lamb with the spice blend *ras el hanout* brought complexity.

- 4 teaspoons extra-virgin olive oil, divided
- 4 ounces ground lamb
- 1¼ teaspoons ras el hanout, divided
- ⅛ teaspoon table salt
- ⅛ teaspoon pepper
- 1 pound eggplant, cut into ½-inch pieces
- 1 small onion, chopped fine
- 2 garlic cloves, minced
- 2 cups chicken broth
- 1 (14.5-ounce) can diced tomatoes, drained
- 1 teaspoon lemon juice
- 3 tablespoons minced fresh cilantro

1. Heat 2 teaspoons oil in 12-inch nonstick skillet over medium-high heat until shimmering. Add lamb, ¼ teaspoon ras el hanout, salt, and pepper and cook, breaking up meat with wooden spoon, until lamb is lightly browned, about 3 minutes. Using slotted spoon, transfer lamb to small bowl; set aside until ready to serve. Pour off all but 2 teaspoons fat from saucepan. (If necessary, add oil to equal 2 teaspoons.) Add eggplant to fat left in skillet and cook, stirring occasionally, until eggplant is tender and deeply browned, 8 to 10 minutes. Transfer to second bowl; set aside until ready to serve.

2. Heat remaining 2 teaspoons oil in large saucepan over medium heat until shimmering. Add onion and cook until softened, about 5 minutes. Stir in garlic and remaining 1 teaspoon ras el hanout and cook until fragrant, about 30 seconds. Stir in broth, tomatoes, and all but 1 cup eggplant and bring to simmer. Reduce heat to low, cover, and simmer gently until eggplant is softened, about 15 minutes.

3. Process soup in blender until smooth, about 1 minute. Return soup to clean saucepan and bring to brief simmer, adjusting consistency with hot water as needed. Stir in lemon juice and season with salt and pepper to taste. Divide soup among individual serving bowls, then top with lamb, remaining 1 cup eggplant, and cilantro. Serve.

■ **CUSTOMIZE IT**

Add crunch	Slivered toasted almonds would lend delicious crunch to this bowl.
Instead of lamb	Ground pork or beef would work.

Chicken Tortilla Soup with Chard

Serves 6 | Calories per Serving: 320

Why This Recipe Works A flavorful broth, tender chicken, subtle heat, and crispy tortilla strips make chicken tortilla soup a Mexican classic. Swiss chard, though unusual, added satisfying bulk to our soup. Chipotle chiles and adobo sauce lent warm, spicy heat; for more heat, use the larger quantity of adobo sauce. The real star of this soup is the Crispy Tortilla Strips, which take just a few minutes in the oven and soften slightly in the broth.

1 tablespoon vegetable oil
1 onion, chopped fine
¼ teaspoon table salt
1 (14.5-ounce) can diced tomatoes, drained
1 tablespoon tomato paste
2 teaspoons minced canned chipotle chile in adobo plus 1–3 teaspoons adobo sauce

2 garlic cloves, minced
8 cups chicken broth
1½ pounds boneless, skinless chicken breasts, trimmed
12 ounces Swiss chard, stemmed and chopped coarse
1 recipe Crispy Tortilla Strips (page 215)

1. Heat oil in Dutch oven over medium heat until shimmering. Add onion and salt and cook until just beginning to soften, about 3 minutes. Stir in tomatoes, tomato paste, and chipotle plus adobo sauce and cook until onion is softened and mixture has darkened, 5 to 7 minutes. Stir in garlic and cook until fragrant, about 30 seconds.

2. Add broth and chicken to pot, cover, and bring to boil. Reduce heat to medium-low and simmer until chicken registers 160 degrees, 12 to 14 minutes. Transfer chicken to plate and let cool slightly. Meanwhile, stir chard into broth and cook until chard is mostly tender, about 5 minutes.

3. Once chicken is cool enough to handle, shred into bite-size pieces using 2 forks. Stir chicken into broth and cook until chicken is warmed through and chard is fully tender, about 5 minutes. Season soup with salt to taste.

4. Divide tortilla strips among individual serving bowls and ladle soup over top. Serve.

■ CUSTOMIZE IT

Instead of Swiss chard	Use baby spinach and stir it into the soup with the shredded chicken.
Kick it up a notch	Avocado, *queso fresco*, and fresh cilantro all pair perfectly with the flavors of this soup.
Simplify the tortillas	Use store-bought tortilla strips in place of homemade.
Make it heartier	Canned beans, or even sautéed corn or zucchini, would add bulk.

Black Bean Soup

Serves 4 to 6 | Calories per Serving: 300

Why This Recipe Works An all-time favorite for both lunch and dinner, black bean soup can be customized in nearly endless ways with toppings. For a simple black bean soup with balanced sweet, spicy, and smoky flavors, we avoided the long process of soaking and simmering dried beans by going straight for canned. Pureeing a portion of the beans gave our soup body, while a base of aromatics—garlic, oregano, cumin, and chili powder—gave it depth; dried porcini mushrooms brought umami flavor. To finish this soup with a little bite, we added red onion and cilantro. A drizzle of Creamy Avocado Dressing, which comes together quickly in a food processor, added richness and bright acid to liven up the soup.

4 (15-ounce) cans black beans, rinsed, divided

3 cups chicken or vegetable broth, divided

1 tablespoon vegetable oil

1 onion, chopped fine

1 red bell pepper, stemmed, seeded, and chopped fine

6 garlic cloves, minced

1 tablespoon minced fresh oregano or 1 teaspoon dried

¼ ounce dried porcini mushrooms, rinsed and minced

½ teaspoon ground cumin

½ teaspoon chili powder

½ cup minced fresh cilantro

1 recipe Creamy Avocado Dressing (page 224)

½ cup thinly sliced red onion

1. Process 2 cups beans and 1 cup broth in blender until smooth, about 10 seconds; set aside.

2. Combine oil, onion, and bell pepper in Dutch oven and cook over medium-high heat until vegetables are softened and lightly browned, 5 to 7 minutes. Stir in garlic, oregano, mushrooms, cumin, and chili powder and cook until fragrant, about 30 seconds. Stir in remaining 2 cups broth, scraping up any browned bits.

3. Stir in pureed beans and remaining beans and simmer until flavors meld, about 15 minutes. Stir in cilantro and season with salt and pepper to taste. Divide among individual serving bowls, then top with dressing and red onion. Serve.

■ CUSTOMIZE IT

Add crunch	Plantain chips would make an unexpected but fantastic topping.
Kick it up a notch	Instead of raw red onion, add Quick Sweet and Spicy Pickled Red Onions (page 217) for tangy, spicy crunch.
Simplify the dressing	Dollop on yogurt or sour cream and add sliced avocado.

Thai-Style Hot and Sour Soup

Serves 4 | Calories per Serving: 220

Why This Recipe Works The hot and sour Thai soup known as *tom yum* is a bold example of the energetic flavors for which Thai cuisine is famous. To create a quick, pantry-friendly version, we substituted an easy-to-find jalapeño for traditional Thai chiles and lime juice for harder-to-find makrut lime leaves. To enhance the potent shrimp flavor in our soup, we saved the shrimp shells to simmer in a combination of chicken broth and water along with plentiful aromatics for an intensely flavorful broth with thorough shrimp flavor, which we balanced with fish sauce and sugar. We then strained and poured the broth over vermicelli rice noodles and topped the soup with a final burst of tart lime juice and fresh cilantro. To smash the ginger pieces, use the flat side of a chef's knife.

4 ounces rice vermicelli noodles

3 cups chicken or vegetable broth

3 cups water

1 pound large shrimp (26 to 30 per pound), peeled, deveined, and tails removed, shells reserved

8 ounces cremini mushrooms, stemmed and quartered, stems reserved

2 tomatoes, cored and chopped coarse, divided

1 jalapeño chile, stemmed, seeded, and sliced into ¼-inch-thick rings, divided

2 sprigs fresh cilantro plus ¼ cup chopped

2 tablespoons fish sauce

2 garlic cloves, lightly crushed and peeled

1 (½-inch) piece ginger, peeled, halved, and smashed

1 teaspoon sugar

3 tablespoons lime juice, plus lime wedges for serving (2 limes)

1. Bring 2 quarts water to boil in large saucepan. Off heat, add noodles and let sit until tender, about 5 minutes. Drain noodles and rinse with cold water until water runs clear, shaking to remove excess water. Set aside.

2. Bring broth, 3 cups water, shrimp shells, mushroom stems, half of tomatoes, half of jalapeño rings, 2 sprigs cilantro, fish sauce, garlic, ginger, and sugar to boil in now-empty saucepan. Reduce heat to low, cover, and simmer gently for 20 minutes.

3. Strain broth through fine-mesh strainer set over large bowl, pushing on solids to extract as much liquid as possible. Return broth to again-empty saucepan and bring to simmer over medium-high heat. Add quartered mushrooms and remaining jalapeño rings and cook for 2 minutes. Stir in shrimp and cook for 1 minute. Off heat, stir in lime juice and season with salt and pepper to taste.

4. Divide noodles and remaining chopped tomatoes among individual serving bowls and ladle soup over top. Top with chopped cilantro. Serve with lime wedges.

■ CUSTOMIZE IT

Instead of cilantro	Fresh basil, or a combination of basil and cilantro, would add herbal depth to this soup.
Kick it up a notch	Thai Chili Jam (page 221) is outstandingly delicious and would lend sweet, savory, spicy flavor to this soup.

Hearty Cabbage Soup

Serves 2 | Calories per Serving: 420

Why This Recipe Works Assertive aromatics and herbs give cabbage an unexpected star quality in this satisfying soup, which makes for a hearty meal for two thanks to the addition of creamy red potatoes, ground chicken, and bacon, which we crisped and reserved to use as a topping. Caraway seeds brought out the sweetness of the cabbage, and smoked paprika and fresh thyme added depth and complexity. A dollop of yogurt served as a tangy counterpoint to the soup's mild sweetness, and a final sprinkling of fresh dill enhanced the caraway's flavor. Be sure to use ground chicken and not ground chicken breast (also labeled 99 percent fat-free) in this recipe.

2 slices bacon, chopped
4 ounces ground chicken
1 small onion, chopped fine
½ teaspoon caraway seeds, toasted
2 garlic cloves, minced
½ teaspoon minced fresh thyme or
⅛ teaspoon dried
¼ teaspoon hot smoked paprika

¼ cup dry white wine
½ small head green cabbage, cored and cut into ¾-inch pieces (3 cups)
2½ cups chicken broth
8 ounces red potatoes, unpeeled and cut into ¾-inch pieces
¼ cup plain Greek yogurt
2 tablespoons minced fresh dill

1. Cook bacon in large saucepan over medium-high heat until crisp, about 5 minutes. Using slotted spoon, transfer bacon to paper towel–lined plate; set aside until ready to serve.

2. Pour off all but 1 tablespoon fat from saucepan. (If necessary, add oil to equal 1 tablespoon.) Add chicken, onion, and caraway seeds to saucepan and cook over medium heat, breaking up chicken with wooden spoon, until chicken is no longer pink and onion is softened, about 5 minutes.

3. Stir in garlic, thyme, and paprika and cook until fragrant, about 30 seconds. Stir in wine, scraping up any browned bits, and cook until nearly evaporated, about 30 seconds. Stir in cabbage and broth and bring to simmer. Reduce heat to medium-low, cover, and cook for 15 minutes. Stir in potatoes and cook until vegetables are tender, 15 to 20 minutes. Season soup with salt and pepper to taste.

4. Divide soup among individual serving bowls then top with bacon, yogurt, and dill. Serve.

■ **CUSTOMIZE IT**

Add crunch	Croutons, either homemade (page 215) or store-bought, would add buttery crunch to this bowl.
Kick it up a notch	Sauerkraut would make for a nice additional layer of tangy flavor.

Quinoa and Vegetable Stew

Serves 2 | Calories per Serving: 350

Why This Recipe Works Hearty, nutritious quinoa isn't just a great base for grain bowls. Here it's the perfect starting point for a stew that holds an array of lively toppings. Drawing inspiration from South American quinoa stew, we spiced our version with paprika, garlic, cumin, and coriander, plus onion and red bell pepper, for a flavor-packed base. We then added broth and potatoes, and once the potatoes started to soften we added the quinoa and cooked it just enough to release starch and give the stew body, stirring in corn toward the end to prevent overcooking. A few easy toppers—*queso fresco* and cilantro—gave this bowl bright, fresh flavor. This stew tends to thicken as it sits, so if you're planning to make it in advance, add more warm broth or water as needed before serving to loosen. We like the convenience of prewashed quinoa, but if you buy unwashed quinoa, be sure to rinse it before cooking to remove its bitter protective coating (called saponin).

1 tablespoon vegetable oil

1 small onion, chopped fine

½ red bell pepper, stemmed, seeded, and cut into ½-inch pieces

2 garlic cloves, minced

1 teaspoon paprika

¾ teaspoon ground coriander

½ teaspoon ground cumin

2 cups chicken or vegetable broth

½ cup water, plus extra as needed

6 ounces red potatoes, unpeeled and cut into ½-inch pieces

⅓ cup prewashed white quinoa

⅓ cup fresh or frozen corn

1 ounce queso fresco, crumbled (¼ cup)

3 tablespoons minced fresh cilantro

Lime wedges

1. Heat oil in large saucepan over medium heat until shimmering. Add onion, bell pepper, garlic, paprika, coriander, and cumin and cook until vegetables are softened and spices are fragrant, about 5 minutes. Stir in broth, water, and potatoes, scraping up any browned bits with wooden spoon. Bring to simmer and cook for 10 minutes.

2. Stir in quinoa and simmer for 8 minutes. Stir in corn and continue to simmer until vegetables and quinoa are just tender, 6 to 8 minutes. Adjust consistency of soup with hot water as needed then season with salt and pepper to taste.

3. Divide soup among individual serving bowls, then top with queso fresco and cilantro. Serve with lime wedges.

■ CUSTOMIZE IT

Kick it up a notch	Avocado would add creamy richness.
Instead of queso fresco	Feta cheese makes an excellent replacement for queso fresco.
Make it heartier	For a little bit of bulk, frozen peas make a nice addition.

Kimchi Beef-Noodle Soup

Serves 2 | Calories per Serving: 590

Why This Recipe Works Though traditionally used as a condiment, tangy, spicy fermented kimchi makes a fantastic base for a soup since it brings so much flavor to the pot. We enhanced the kimchi's inherent umami with meaty steak tips. Doubling up on kimchi by incorporating ⅓ cup of its brine allowed its bold flavor to shine in our soup, while a combination of beef broth, mirin, soy sauce, and ginger gave us a balanced, aromatic broth. To make the soup hearty, we added tender rice noodles. Make sure to save the kimchi brine when draining and measuring the kimchi. Sirloin steak tips, also known as flap meat, can be sold as whole steaks, cubes, and strips. To ensure uniform pieces, we prefer to buy whole steaks and cut them ourselves.

6 ounces (¼-inch-wide) rice noodles
6 ounces sirloin steak tips, trimmed and cut into ½-inch pieces
⅛ teaspoon table salt
⅛ teaspoon pepper
1 teaspoon vegetable oil
2 teaspoons grated fresh ginger

1½ cups beef broth
1 cup water
⅓ cup mirin
¾ cup drained kimchi, chopped coarse, plus ⅓ cup kimchi brine
1½ teaspoons soy sauce
2 scallions, sliced thin

1. Pour 2 quarts boiling water over noodles in bowl and stir to separate. Let noodles soak until soft and pliable but not fully tender, stirring once halfway through soaking, 8 to 10 minutes. Drain noodles and rinse with cold water until water runs clear, shaking to remove excess water. While noodles soak, pat beef dry with paper towels and sprinkle with salt and pepper. Heat oil in large saucepan over medium-high heat until just smoking. Add beef and cook until well browned on all sides, 6 to 8 minutes.

2. Stir in ginger and cook until fragrant, about 30 seconds. Stir in broth, water, mirin, kimchi brine, and soy sauce, scraping up any browned bits, then bring to boil. Reduce heat to low, cover, and simmer until meat is tender, about 25 minutes. Stir in noodles, return to boil, and cook until noodles are tender, about 1 minute. Season with salt and pepper to taste.

3. Divide noodles, beef, and broth among individual serving bowls then top with kimchi and sprinkle with scallions. Serve.

■ CUSTOMIZE IT

Make it heartier	Stir in cubed tofu for extra protein.
Instead of rice noodles	Fully cooked udon, ramen, or fresh Chinese noodles would also work.

North African Vegetable and Bean Stew

Serves 6 | **Calories per Serving: 350**

Why This Recipe Works Boldly aromatic North African harissa packs a flavorful punch, so to create a substantial stew that enhanced the harissa's flavor we turned to hearty chickpeas, tender carrots, earthy Swiss chard, and ditalini pasta to build a bulky base. Adding garlic, cinnamon, and tomato paste to our broth enhanced the flavor of the harissa, and a topping of fresh parsley and Greek yogurt added bright, tangy bite.

1 tablespoon extra-virgin olive oil
1 onion, chopped fine
8 ounces Swiss chard, ½ cup stems chopped fine, leaves cut into ½-inch pieces
1 recipe Harissa, divided (page 222)
4 garlic cloves, minced
¼ teaspoon ground cinnamon

2 tablespoons tomato paste
7 cups chicken or vegetable broth
2 carrots, peeled and cut into ½-inch pieces
2 (15-ounce) cans chickpeas, rinsed
½ cup ditalini pasta
⅓ cup chopped fresh parsley
6 tablespoons Greek yogurt

1. Heat oil in Dutch oven over medium heat until shimmering. Add onion and chard stems and cook until softened, about 5 minutes. Stir in ¼ cup harissa, garlic, and cinnamon and cook until fragrant, about 30 seconds. Stir in tomato paste and cook for 1 minute.

2. Stir in broth and carrots, scraping up any browned bits, and bring to boil. Reduce heat to medium-low and simmer gently for 10 minutes. Stir in chard leaves, chickpeas, and pasta and simmer until vegetables and pasta are tender, 10 to 15 minutes.

3. Off heat, using potato masher, gently mash half of chickpeas in pot. Stir to recombine and season with salt and pepper to taste. Divide soup among individual serving bowls, then top with remaining ¼ cup harissa, parsley, and yogurt. Serve.

■ CUSTOMIZE IT

Add crunch	Pita Crumble (page 214) or crumbled store-bought pita chips would pair perfectly with the flavors of this bowl.
Instead of chickpeas	Butter beans make for a delicious replacement for the chickpeas.
Instead of ditalini	Elbow macaroni also works well in this soup.
Simplify the harissa	Store-bought harissa also works (you'll need ½ cup), but the spiciness can vary by brand.

Ramen Zoodle Bowl

Serves 2 | Calories per Serving: 310

Why This Recipe Works For a lighter spin on a Japanese ramen bowl, we swapped out traditional ramen noodles for zucchini noodles, which turned perfectly tender after just one minute in the hot broth. For a simple broth full of rich flavors, we infused store-bought chicken broth with sesame oil, miso, and ginger. Our spinach required a few more seconds than the zucchini noodles to wilt, so we stirred it in right at the end of cooking the broth. To top our bowl, enoki mushrooms were ideal as they can be eaten raw but turn meltingly tender from the heat of the broth. Use vegetable broth to make this dish vegetarian. Enoki mushrooms can be hard to find if you don't have a well-stocked supermarket; if you can't find them, we recommend doubling the amount of shiitake mushrooms you cook in step 1.

- 1 tablespoon vegetable oil
- 4 ounces shiitake mushrooms, stemmed and sliced thin
- 3 scallions, white parts cut into 1-inch lengths, green parts sliced thin
- 2 tablespoons white miso
- 2 teaspoons grated fresh ginger

- 3 cups chicken or vegetable broth
- 1 cup water
- 2 ounces (2 cups) baby spinach
- 2 tablespoons toasted sesame oil
- 12 ounces spiralized zucchini noodles (see page 193)
- 2 ounces enoki mushrooms, trimmed

1. Heat vegetable oil in large saucepan over medium heat until just smoking. Add shiitake mushrooms and scallion whites and cook until lightly browned and tender, about 5 minutes.

2. Stir in miso and ginger and cook until fragrant, about 30 seconds. Stir in broth and water and bring to simmer. Stir in spinach and cook until just wilted, about 15 seconds. Stir in sesame oil and season with salt and pepper to taste.

3. Divide noodles among individual serving bowls and ladle hot broth over top; let sit for 1 minute. Top with enoki mushrooms and scallion greens. Serve.

■ CUSTOMIZE IT

Make it heartier	Easy-Peel Soft-Cooked Eggs (page 199) or cubed tofu make for easy protein additions. Or, go crazy and add both!
Instead of zucchini noodles	Ramen noodles will also work in this bowl. You'll need to fully cook them separately in boiling water (discarding the flavor packet).
Kick it up a notch	Asian chili-garlic sauce is a simple store-bought addition that will add spicy flavor to this bowl. Sprinkle on crumbled nori for extra umami.

Acquacotta Bowl

Serves 2 | Calories per Serving: 490

Why This Recipe Works   Its name may translate as "cooked water," but this Italian relative of minestrone is a robust and rustic one-bowl meal. We started with a base of creamy cannellini beans, tender fennel, and faintly bitter escarole. For a quick but flavorful broth, we amped up store-bought chicken broth with a *soffritto*, a mixture of sautéed onion, celery, and garlic. Aromatic fresh oregano gave our soup a distinctively herby taste. A topping of toasted bread and additional fresh escarole made the soup even heartier and allowed us to sop up all the delicious broth.

3 tablespoons extra-virgin olive oil, divided
1 small onion, chopped fine
1 celery rib, minced
2 garlic cloves, minced
¼ teaspoon red pepper flakes
2 tomatoes, cored and cut into ½-inch pieces, divided
3 cups chicken or vegetable broth

½ small fennel bulb, stalks discarded, bulb halved, cored, and cut into ½-inch pieces
1 (15-ounce) can cannellini beans, rinsed
½ small head escarole (6 ounces), trimmed and cut into ½-inch pieces, divided
1 teaspoon minced fresh oregano
2 (½-inch-thick) slices rustic white bread

1. Heat 2 tablespoons oil in large saucepan over medium heat until shimmering. Add onion, celery, garlic, and pepper flakes and cook until vegetables are lightly browned, 6 to 8 minutes. Stir in half of tomatoes and cook, stirring occasionally, until tomatoes break down and mixture begins to brown, about 5 minutes.

2. Stir in broth and fennel, scraping up any browned bits, and bring to simmer. Reduce heat to medium-low and simmer until fennel begins to soften, 5 to 7 minutes. Stir in beans and all but 1 cup escarole and cook until fennel is tender, 5 to 7 minutes. Off heat, stir in oregano and season with salt and pepper to taste.

3. Meanwhile, adjust oven rack 6 inches from broiler element and heat broiler. Place bread on aluminum foil–lined rimmed baking sheet and drizzle with remaining 1 tablespoon oil. Broil until bread is deep golden brown.

4. Divide soup among individual serving bowls then top with toasted bread, remaining 1 cup escarole, and remaining tomato. Serve.

■ CUSTOMIZE IT

For extra flavor	Grated Pecorino Romano adds salty bite (Parmesan works, too). For more fennel flavor, mince and sprinkle the fennel fronds over the top.
Make it heartier	Eggs are common additions to acquacotta. Add a poached egg to each bowl for a deliciously runny yolk.
Instead of cannellini beans	Chickpeas would work well as a replacement.

Vegetable Shabu-Shabu Bowl

Serves 4 | Calories per Serving: 360

Why This Recipe Works Shabu-shabu is a hot-pot favorite in which meat or tofu and an array of vegetables are simmered in broth and served with udon noodles. We wanted a version without the meat (or the hot pot). The traditional broth is made from a combination of kombu seaweed and bonito (tuna) flakes. After a good deal of testing, we found that we preferred the delicate fishy depth from a second variety of seaweed (wakame), rice wine, fish sauce, and sugar over the traditional bonito. Shabu-shabu typically includes carrots, napa cabbage or bok choy, enoki or shiitake mushrooms, tofu, and chrysanthemum leaves. Luckily, the hard-to-find chrysanthemum leaves weren't missed, and we found that we preferred bok choy to cabbage and the fuller flavor of shiitake mushrooms. Though we often prefer fresh, we found that dried noodles worked just as well in this soup. For a fully vegetarian version, replace the fish sauce with Bragg liquid aminos.

6 ounces dried udon noodles	3 heads baby bok choy (4 ounces each), sliced ⅛ inch thick
½ ounce kombu, rinsed	3 carrots, peeled and sliced ⅛ inch thick
½ ounce wakame, rinsed	14 ounces soft tofu, cut into ½-inch pieces
½ cup mirin	8 ounces shiitake mushrooms, stemmed and sliced thin
¼ cup fish sauce	
1½ teaspoons sugar	

1. Bring 2 quarts water to boil in large saucepan. Add udon noodles and cook, stirring often, until tender. Drain noodles and set aside.

2. Bring 9 cups water, kombu, and wakame to brief boil in large pot over medium heat. Off heat, discard seaweed. Stir in mirin, fish sauce, and sugar and bring to simmer over medium heat. Stir in bok choy and carrots and simmer until crisp-tender, 2 to 4 minutes. Season with salt and pepper to taste.

3. Divide tofu, mushrooms, and noodles among individual serving bowls and ladle broth over top. Serve.

■ CUSTOMIZE IT

Instead of udon	Soba noodles would also work.
Kick it up a notch	Sesame Sauce (page 220) would make for a perfect final addition.

bowl basics

TOPPINGS

DRESSINGS & SAUCES

grains & noodles

Grains and noodles add heft and make for a versatile base for a variety of toppings. Many whole grains are high in fiber and protein, making them satisfying options for vegetarian meals, and many are easy to cook using a pasta method so you can make them ahead and reheat for quick weeknight bowls. Noodles cook relatively quickly and work well for brothy soup bowls or noodle bowls with flavorful sauces that will cling to the noodles.

MASTER RECIPE FOR GRAINS

To cook the below grains, bring water to boil in large pot. Stir in grain and table salt and cook until tender, following timing below. Drain well. All of these grains can be cooked, cooled, and refrigerated in an airtight container for up to 3 days. If serving immediately, season with salt and pepper to taste.

Reheating Grains

To reheat grains, microwave in covered bowl until hot throughout, fluffing with fork halfway through microwaving, then season with salt and pepper to taste (timing will vary depending on the quantity and type of grains used).

GRAIN	DRY AMOUNT (CUPS)	WATER (QUARTS)	SALT (TEASPOON)	COOKED YIELD (CUPS)	COOKING TIME (MINUTES)
Buckwheat	¾	2	½	2	10 to 12
	1½	4	1	4	
Medium- or coarse-grind bulgur	¾	2	½	2	5
	1½	4	1	4	
Pearl barley	¾	2	½	2	20 to 40
	1½	4	1	4	
Farro	¾	2	½	2	15 to 30
	1½	4	1	4	
Freekeh	¾	2	½	2	30 to 45
	1½	4	1	4	
Black rice	¾	2	½	2	20 to 25
	1½	4	1	4	
Long-grain brown rice	¾	2	½	2	25 to 30
	1½	4	1	4	
Long-grain white rice	¾	2	½	2	10 to 15
	1½	4	1	4	
Wild rice	¾	2	½	2	35 to 40
	1½	4	1	4	
Oat berries	¾	2	½	1½	30 to 40
	1½	4	1	3	
Wheat berries	¾	4	½	1½	60 to 70
	1½	4	1	3	

SIMPLE WHITE RICE PILAF

Makes about 2 cups, enough for 2 bowls

This easy pilaf method adds rich, flavorful depth to fluffy, make-ahead rice that requires just a little more effort than standard boiling. You will need a small saucepan with a tight-fitting lid.

- 1 tablespoon extra-virgin olive oil, vegetable oil, or unsalted butter
- ¾ cup basmati, jasmine, or other long-grain white rice, rinsed
- 1¼ cups water or broth
- ¼ teaspoon table salt

1. Heat oil in medium saucepan over medium heat until shimmering. Stir in rice and cook until edges of grains begin to turn translucent, about 2 minutes. Stir in water and salt and bring to boil. Reduce heat to low, cover, and simmer until all liquid is absorbed, 18 to 22 minutes.

2. Off heat, remove lid, place folded clean dish towel over saucepan, then replace lid. Let rice sit for 10 minutes, then gently fluff with fork. Season with salt and pepper to taste. (Rice can be refrigerated for up to 3 days.)

VARIATION
Big Batch Simple White Rice Pilaf

Makes about 7 cups, enough for 7 bowls

Increase rice to 2 cups, water to 3 cups, and salt to 1 teaspoon. Cook the rice in a large saucepan instead of a medium saucepan.

....

HANDS-OFF BAKED BROWN RICE

Makes about 2 cups, enough for 2 bowls

For a basic brown rice recipe that was entirely hands-off, we turned to the oven. The test kitchen's preferred loaf pan measures 8½ by 4½ inches; if you use a 9 by 5-inch loaf pan, start checking for doneness 5 minutes early.

- 1¼ cups boiling water or broth
- ¾ cup long-grain, medium-grain, or short-grain brown rice, rinsed
- 2 teaspoons extra-virgin olive oil, vegetable oil, or unsalted butter
- ¼ teaspoon table salt

1. Adjust oven rack to middle position and heat oven to 375 degrees. Combine boiling water, rice, oil, and salt in 8½ by 4½-inch loaf pan. Cover pan tightly with double layer of aluminum foil. Bake until rice is tender and no water remains, 45 to 55 minutes.

2. Remove pan from oven and fluff rice with fork, scraping up any rice that has stuck to bottom. Cover pan with clean dish towel, then re-cover loosely with foil. Let rice sit for 10 minutes. Season with salt and pepper to taste. (Rice can be refrigerated for up to 3 days.)

VARIATION
Big Batch Hands-Off Baked Brown Rice

Makes about 4 cups, enough for 4 bowls

Increase boiling water to 2⅓ cups, rice to 1½ cups, and salt to ½ teaspoon. Use an 8-inch square baking dish instead of an 8½ by 4½-inch loaf pan. Increase baking time in step 1 to about 1 hour.

Try one of these combinations, or use the ideas as inspiration. **Top:** Freekeh (page 189), Roasted Sweet Potatoes (page 209), arugula, jalapeño, goat cheese, pomegranate seeds, Pomegranate-Honey Vinaigrette (page 219) **Bottom:** Fresh Chinese noodles (page 193), shredded chicken (page 194), cucumber, snap peas, torn nori sheets, Peanut-Sesame Sauce (page 222)

QUINOA PILAF

Makes about 2 cups, enough for 2 bowls

We love quinoa as a base for a hearty bowl, and it also works surprisingly well as a salad topping, as in our Quinoa Taco Salad Bowl (page 24). For guaranteed tender, flavorful quinoa, we turned to the same pilaf method we use for rice, toasting the quinoa in a skillet before adding our liquid to help its nutty flavor develop. If you buy unwashed quinoa (or if you are unsure whether it's been washed), be sure to rinse it before cooking to remove its bitter protective coating (called saponin).

¾ cup prewashed white quinoa
1¼ cups water or broth
¼ teaspoon table salt

1. Cook quinoa in medium saucepan over medium-high heat, stirring frequently, until very fragrant and makes continuous popping sound, 5 to 7 minutes. Stir in water and salt and bring to simmer. Reduce heat to low, cover, and simmer until quinoa is tender and water is absorbed, 18 to 22 minutes, stirring once halfway through cooking.

2. Remove pot from heat and let sit, covered, for 10 minutes, then gently fluff with fork. Season with salt and pepper to taste. (Quinoa can be refrigerated for up to 3 days.)

VARIATION
Big Batch Quinoa Pilaf

Makes about 4 cups, enough for 4 bowls
Increase quinoa to 1½ cups, water to 1¾ cups, and salt to ½ teaspoon. Increase covered time in step 2 to 18 to 20 minutes.

CREAMY PARMESAN POLENTA

Makes about 2 cups, enough for 2 bowls

Polenta makes for a sturdy bowl base that can take on toppings with earthy, nutty flavors like butternut squash and pistachio dukkah (page 211), or bold, bitter flavors like broccoli rabe, as in our Polenta Bowl with Broccoli Rabe and Fried Eggs (page 101). A pinch of baking soda cut cooking time in half and eliminated the need for stirring, giving us the best quick polenta recipe.

2½ cups water
¼ teaspoon table salt
    Pinch baking soda
½ cup coarse-ground cornmeal
1 ounce Parmesan cheese, grated (½ cup)
1 tablespoon unsalted butter

1. Bring water to boil in small saucepan over medium-high heat. Stir in salt and baking soda. Slowly add cornmeal in steady stream, stirring constantly. Bring mixture to boil, stirring constantly, about 30 seconds. Reduce heat to lowest possible setting and cover.

2. After 5 minutes, whisk cornmeal to smooth out any lumps, making sure to scrape down sides and bottom of saucepan. Cover and continue to cook, without stirring, until cornmeal is tender but slightly al dente, 8 to 10 minutes longer. (Polenta should be loose and barely hold its shape; it will continue to thicken as it cools.)

3. Off heat, stir in Parmesan and butter and season with salt and pepper to taste. Cover and let sit for 5 minutes. (Polenta can be refrigerated for up to 3 days.)

VARIATION
Big Batch Creamy Parmesan Polenta

Makes about 6 cups, enough for 6 bowls
Increase water to 7½ cups, salt to 1½ teaspoons, cornmeal to 1½ cups, Parmesan to 2 ounces, and butter to 2 tablespoons. Cook the polenta in a large saucepan instead of a small saucepan. Increase the covered cooking time in step 2 to 25 minutes.

pasta & noodles 101

DRIED WHEAT PASTA, SOBA NOODLES, AND FRESH NOODLES

To cook noodles, bring 2–4 quarts of water to a boil in a large pot. Add noodles and cook, stirring often until al dente or tender, depending on the application. Drain well. To ensure tender, not mushy noodles we often rinse cooked noodles with cold water to halt the cooking process. For warm bowls, we prefer to cook the noodles just before preparing the bowl, but for chilled or room-temperature bowls you could make the noodles ahead and refrigerate.

Dried Wheat Pasta

Use 6 ounces of dried noodles for 2 bowls, or 1 pound for 4 to 6 bowls. Add salt with the noodles.

Soba Noodles

Soba noodles tend to clump together once chilled, so we recommend tossing them with a small amount of oil before refrigerating. Drained and cooled noodles can be refrigerated for up to 2 days.

Fresh Noodles

Fresh Chinese noodles are more starchy and chewy than dried noodles. Udon noodles are made with a highly elastic dough that yields thick, chewy noodles. Fresh noodles often cook in just a few minutes.

VEGETABLE NOODLES

You can buy vegetable noodles fresh or frozen at most supermarkets, but we find that they can be tough and dry and prefer to make them ourselves with a spiralizer. Zucchini, summer squash, carrots, and beets are some of the common vegetables you'll see spiralized, but celery root, parsnips, rutabaga, and sweet potatoes can also be spiralized.

Beets

Use beets that are at least 1½ inches in diameter. Spiralized beets can be added raw to salads or roasted for a warm dish.

Carrots

Use carrots that are at least ¾ inch wide at the thinnest end and 1½ inches wide at the thickest end. Spiralized carrots can be used raw in salads or roasted for warm dishes.

Summer Squash and Zucchini

Use smaller, in-season summer squash and zucchini, which have thinner skins and fewer seeds. Zucchini and summer squash noodles taste great raw in some applications, but they can also be served cooked. Sauté them or add them to soup at the very end of cooking to cook them through gently.

SPIRALIZING VEGETABLE NOODLES

1. Trim vegetable so it will fit on prongs.

2. Secure vegetable between prongs and blade surface. Spiralize by turning crank.

3. Pull noodles straight and cut into desired length.

proteins

Without enough protein, a meal simply doesn't feel like a meal, so we wanted to offer a selection of basic proteins that would make a great addition to any bowl. Many of these proteins can be made ahead and refrigerated until you're ready to prepare your bowl. We also include a few homemade spice rubs in this section to easily change up the flavor of your protein.

PERFECT POACHED CHICKEN

Makes 2 cups shredded cooked chicken, enough for 2 bowls

Simple poached chicken breast makes for a perfect protein topping thanks to its versatility to adapt to many different flavor profiles. It's important that the chicken breasts are similar in size so that they cook at the same rate. You can poach up to 4 chicken breasts at one time using this recipe. Brining the chicken in the poaching liquid helps it to absorb extra flavor and turn supertender, but to speed up the recipe you could skip the 30-minute brining.

- ½ cup soy sauce
- ¼ cup table salt
- 2 (6-ounce) boneless, skinless chicken breasts, trimmed and pounded to even thickness

1. Whisk 4 quarts water, soy sauce, and salt together in Dutch oven until salt is dissolved. Arrange chicken, skinned side up, in steamer basket, submerge in brine, and let sit at room temperature for 30 minutes.

2. Heat pot over medium heat, stirring liquid occasionally to even out hot spots, until water registers 175 degrees, 15 to 20 minutes. Turn off heat, cover pot, remove from burner, and let sit until chicken registers 160 degrees, 17 to 22 minutes.

3. Transfer chicken to cutting board, tent with aluminum foil, and let rest for 5 minutes. Slice or shred chicken as desired. (Chicken can be refrigerated for up to 2 days.)

SEARED CHICKEN BREASTS

Makes 2 cups chopped cooked chicken, enough for 2 bowls

This simple cooking method helps the chicken stay moist and tender on the inside and develop flavorful browning on the outside. You will need a 10-inch skillet with a tight-fitting lid for this recipe. You can easily double this recipe; double the amount of chicken, salt, and pepper and use a 12-inch skillet instead of a 10-inch skillet.

- 2 (6-ounce) boneless, skinless chicken breasts, trimmed and pounded to even thickness
- ¼ teaspoon table salt
- ⅛ teaspoon pepper
- 1 teaspoon extra-virgin olive oil or vegetable oil
- ¼ cup water

Pat chicken dry with paper towels and sprinkle with salt and pepper. Heat oil in 10-inch skillet over medium-high heat until just smoking. Brown chicken well on first side, about 6 minutes. Flip chicken, add water, and cover. Reduce heat to medium-low and continue to cook until chicken registers 160 degrees, 5 to 7 minutes. Transfer chicken to cutting board, tent with aluminum foil, and let rest for 5 minutes. Slice or shred chicken as desired. (Chicken can be refrigerated for up to 2 days.)

ROAST PORK TENDERLOIN

Makes enough for 2 bowls

For a flavorful weeknight bowl, roast pork tenderloin makes for a surprisingly easy protein option—it can not only be sliced and fanned atop a bowl but also shredded (much faster than braising) as in our Pork Mojo Quinoa Bowl (page 85). You can cook 2 pork tenderloins using this recipe; double the amount of salt and pepper used for seasoning.

- 1 (12-ounce) pork tenderloin, trimmed
- ¼ teaspoon table salt
- ⅛ teaspoon pepper
- 1 teaspoon extra-virgin olive oil or vegetable oil

1. Adjust oven rack to lower-middle position and heat oven to 450 degrees. Pat tenderloin dry with paper towels and sprinkle with salt and pepper. Heat oil in 12-inch ovensafe skillet over medium-high heat until just smoking. Brown tenderloin on all sides, about 10 minutes.

2. Transfer skillet to oven and roast until pork registers 145 degrees, 10 to 15 minutes, flipping meat halfway through roasting.

3. Transfer tenderloin to carving board, tent with aluminum foil, and let rest for 5 minutes. Slice or shred pork as desired. (Pork can be refrigerated for up to 2 days.)

SHREDDING PORK TENDERLOIN

Using 2 forks, shred tenderloin into bite-size pieces.

PAN-SEARED FLANK STEAK

Makes enough for 2 bowls

Inexpensive, full of flavor, and tender when thinly sliced against the grain, flank steak is the perfect cut of beef for topping salad bowls, as in our Steakhouse Salad Bowl (page 36) and Steak Fajita Salad Bowl (page 51), or for topping grain bowls, as in our Skillet Burrito Bowl (page 61). To ensure even cooking and browning, we flipped the steak every minute. You can cook 1 pound of flank steak using this recipe; double the amount of salt and pepper used for seasoning and use a 12-inch skillet instead of a 10-inch skillet.

- 8 ounces flank steak, trimmed
- ¼ teaspoon table salt
- ¼ teaspoon pepper
- 1 teaspoon extra-virgin olive oil or vegetable oil

Pat steak dry with paper towels and sprinkle with salt and pepper. Heat oil in 10-inch nonstick skillet over medium-high heat until just smoking. Add steak and cook, turning every minute, until well browned on both sides and meat registers 130 degrees (for medium), 10 to 14 minutes. Transfer to cutting board, tent with aluminum foil, and let rest for 5 minutes. Slice thin against grain before serving. (Steak can be refrigerated for up to 2 days.)

REHEATING LEFTOVER STEAK

Place leftover steak on a wire rack set in a rimmed baking sheet and warm on the middle rack of a 250-degree oven until the steak registers 110 degrees (roughly 30 minutes for 1½-inch-thick steak, but timing will vary according to thickness and size). Pat the steak dry with a paper towel and heat 1 tablespoon vegetable oil in a 12-inch skillet over high heat until smoking. Sear the steak on both sides until crisp, 60 to 90 seconds per side. Let the steak rest for 5 minutes before serving. After resting, the center should be at medium-rare temperature (125 to 130 degrees).

Try one of these combinations, or use the ideas as inspiration. **Top:** Long-grain Brown Rice (page 189), Oven-Roasted Salmon (page 197), Sautéed Broccoli with Garlic and Thyme (page 203), scallions, Garlic Chips (page 214), Gochujang Sauce (page 221), avocado **Middle:** Bulgur (page 189), Crispy Tempeh (page 198), Roasted Beets (page 202), Creamless Creamy Dressing (page 225), Spanish-Spiced Crispy Chickpeas (page 212) **Bottom:** Carrot Noodles (page 193), shredded chicken (page 194), Marinated Eggplant with Capers and Mint (page 206), Tahini Sauce (page 222), sesame seeds, parsley

SAUTÉED SHRIMP

Makes 1½ cups cooked shrimp, enough for 2–4 bowls

Shrimp's light flavor makes it a delicious topping for a variety of bowls, and as a bonus it tastes great hot or chilled. Try it on a bed of greens, as in our Shrimp and Grapefruit Salad Bowl (page 43); pair it with creamy soup, as in our Curried Coconut Shrimp Soup (page 149); or remake a classic, as in our Shrimp and Grits Bowl (page 102). You can double this recipe: Double the amount of shrimp, salt, pepper, and oil and cook the shrimp in 2 batches.

- 12 ounces extra-large shrimp (21 to 25 per pound), peeled, deveined, and tails removed
- ¼ teaspoon table salt
- ¼ teaspoon pepper
- 1 tablespoon extra-virgin olive oil or vegetable oil

Pat shrimp dry with paper towels and sprinkle with salt and pepper. Heat oil in 12-inch nonstick skillet over medium-high heat until just smoking. Add shrimp in single layer and cook, without stirring, until spotty brown and edges turn pink on bottom side, about 1 minute. Flip shrimp and continue to cook until all but very center is opaque, about 30 seconds; transfer shrimp to plate. (Shrimp can be refrigerated for up to 2 days.)

VARIATIONS
Chipotle Shrimp

Sprinkle shrimp with ¼ teaspoon chipotle chili powder before searing.

Lemony Shrimp

Sprinkle shrimp with 1 teaspoon grated lemon zest before searing.

OVEN-ROASTED SALMON

Makes enough for 2 bowls

Rich, flaky roasted salmon pairs with everything from ginger and cilantro, as in our Forbidden Rice Bowl with Salmon (page 70), to garlic and gochujang (page 221). To ensure uniform pieces of fish that cook at the same rate, buy a whole center-cut fillet and cut it into two pieces. It is important to keep the skin on during cooking; remove it afterward if you choose not to serve it. If cooking wild salmon, cook the fillets until they register 120 degrees (for medium-rare). You can easily double this recipe.

- 1 (12-ounce) center-cut skin-on side of salmon, 1 to 1½ inches thick
- 1 teaspoon extra-virgin olive oil or vegetable oil
- ¼ teaspoon table salt
- ¼ teaspoon pepper

1. Adjust oven rack to lowest position, place rimmed baking sheet on rack, and heat oven to 500 degrees. Cut salmon crosswise into 2 fillets. Make 4 or 5 shallow slashes, about 1 inch apart, on skin side of each fillet, being careful not to cut into flesh. Pat salmon dry with paper towels, rub with oil, and sprinkle with salt and pepper.

2. Reduce oven temperature to 275 degrees and remove baking sheet. Carefully place salmon, skin side down, on baking sheet. Roast until center is still translucent when checked with tip of paring knife and registers 125 degrees (for medium-rare), 9 to 13 minutes; transfer salmon to plate. (Salmon can be refrigerated for up to 2 days.)

VARIATION
Juniper and Fennel Roasted Salmon

While oven preheats, grind 7 juniper berries and ½ teaspoon toasted fennel seeds in spice grinder until coarsely ground, about 30 seconds. Transfer spices to bowl and stir in ½ teaspoon grated orange zest and ¼ teaspoon sugar. Sprinkle salmon with spice mixture and season with salt and pepper to taste after rubbing with oil in step 1.

PAN-SEARED TOFU

Makes 2 cups, enough for 4 bowls

Tofu is more than just a meat replacement—simply seasoned tofu is an incredibly versatile protein option that can pair with a bright sauce like the spicy sriracha in our Sriracha-Lime Tofu Salad Bowl (page 19) or with bold herbs like the Thai basil in our Spicy Basil Noodle Bowl (page 122). This recipe can be easily doubled; you'll need to cook the tofu in batches.

14 ounces soft, firm, or extra-firm tofu, cut into ¾-inch pieces
¼ teaspoon table salt
⅛ teaspoon pepper
2 teaspoons extra-virgin olive oil or vegetable oil

1. Spread tofu over paper towel–lined baking sheet, let drain for 20 minutes, then gently press dry with paper towels. Sprinkle with salt and pepper.

2. Heat oil in 12-inch nonstick skillet over medium-high heat until shimmering. Add tofu and cook until lightly browned, 6 to 8 minutes; transfer to bowl. (Tofu can be refrigerated for up to 2 days.)

CRISPY TEMPEH

Makes 1 cup, enough for 2 bowls

A two-step method—boiling in soy sauce–seasoned water followed by frying—turns typically bland and slightly bitter tempeh into a crunchy umami bomb that will be the star of any bowl it's sprinkled on.

3 tablespoons soy sauce
8 ounces tempeh, crumbled into ¼-inch pieces
1 cup peanut or vegetable oil, for frying

1. Bring 4 cups water and soy sauce to boil in large saucepan. Add tempeh, return to boil, and cook for 10 minutes. Drain tempeh well and wipe saucepan dry with paper towels.

2. Set wire rack in rimmed baking sheet and line with triple layer paper towels. Heat oil in now-empty dry saucepan over medium-high heat until shimmering. Add tempeh and cook until golden brown and crisp, about 12 minutes, adjusting heat as needed if tempeh begins to scorch. Using wire skimmer or slotted spoon, transfer tempeh to prepared sheet to drain, then season with salt and pepper to taste. Serve immediately.

GINGERY STIR-FRIED EDAMAME

Makes 1 cup, enough for 2–4 bowls

Protein-rich edamame makes for a delicious vegan bowl option. You will need a 10-inch nonstick skillet with a tight-fitting lid for this recipe. The recipe can be easily doubled.

1 cup frozen edamame, thawed and patted dry
¼ cup water
1 teaspoon toasted sesame oil
1 scallion, minced
1 teaspoon grated fresh ginger
1 teaspoon soy sauce

1. Cook edamame and water in 10-inch nonstick skillet, covered, until edamame are nearly tender, about 7 minutes. Uncover and continue to cook until water evaporates and edamame are tender, about 2 minutes longer.

2. Push edamame to sides of skillet. Add oil, scallion, and ginger to center and cook, mashing mixture into pan, until fragrant, about 30 seconds. Stir mixture into edamame, then stir in soy sauce; transfer to bowl. (Edamame can be refrigerated for up to 2 days.)

EASY-PEEL HARD-COOKED EGGS

Makes 1–6 eggs

Hard-cooked eggs with their protective, travel-friendly shells are the perfect make-ahead protein for a bowl on the go—especially with this easy-peel method. Be sure to use large eggs that have no cracks and are cold from the refrigerator. You can use this method to cook up to 12 eggs at once; just be sure to use a pot and a steamer basket that's large enough to hold the eggs in a single layer.

  1–6 large eggs

1. Bring 1 inch water to rolling boil in medium saucepan over high heat. Place eggs in steamer basket and transfer basket to saucepan. Cover, reduce heat to medium-low, and cook eggs for 13 minutes.

2. When eggs are almost finished cooking, combine 2 cups ice cubes and 2 cups cold water in bowl. Using tongs or slotted spoon, transfer eggs to ice bath and let sit for 15 minutes. Peel before using. (Hard-cooked eggs can be refrigerated, peeled or unpeeled, for up to 3 days.)

VARIATION
Easy-Peel Soft-Cooked Eggs

Cook over medium-high heat and decrease cooking time to 6½ minutes. In step 2, submerge eggs in ice bath just until cool enough to handle, about 30 seconds.

FRIED EGGS

Makes 2 eggs

A fried egg is the ultimate protein topper for any bowl. And whether you prefer runny yolks or set yolks, our method will produce perfect results every time. You will need a 10-inch nonstick skillet with a tight-fitting lid for this recipe. You can cook up to 4 eggs at a time: Use a 12-inch nonstick skillet, use a second bowl to crack the additional eggs into, and increase oil to 2 teaspoons.

  1 teaspoon extra-virgin olive oil or
     vegetable oil
  2 large eggs
  ⅛ teaspoon table salt
  ⅛ teaspoon pepper

Heat oil in 10-inch nonstick skillet over medium-high heat until shimmering. Crack eggs into small bowl and sprinkle with salt and pepper. Working quickly, pour eggs into pan. Cover and cook for 1 minute. Remove skillet from heat and let sit, covered, 15 to 45 seconds for runny yolks (white around edge of yolk will be barely opaque), 45 to 60 seconds for soft but set yolks, and about 2 minutes for medium-set yolks. Serve immediately.

spice rubs

Use these flavorful spice blends to coat chicken, pork, beef, or even tofu before cooking. All of the blends make about ½ cup and can be stored in an airtight container at room temperature for up to 1 month. Use 1 tablespoon for each pound of boneless protein and 2 tablespoons for each pound of bone-in proteins.

CAJUN-STYLE RUB
Makes ½ cup

You can substitute 2 tablespoons ground celery seeds plus 2 tablespoons salt for the celery salt. For an easy spin on Oven-Roasted Salmon (page 197), sprinkle this spice mixture on after rubbing with oil in step 1.

- 2 tablespoons coriander seeds
- ¼ cup celery salt
- 2 tablespoons paprika
- 1 teaspoon cayenne pepper
- ½ teaspoon ground cinnamon

Process coriander seeds in spice grinder until finely ground, about 30 seconds; transfer to small bowl. Stir in celery salt, paprika, cayenne, and cinnamon.

BARBECUE RUB
Makes ½ cup

Barbecue can mean a lot of different things depending on the region of the country, but this spicy-sweet all-purpose rub is immediately recognizable as "barbecue." Try using this rub on Pan-Seared Flank Steak (page 195) after patting it dry to add spicy-sweet-smoky flavor.

- 3 tablespoons chili powder
- 3 tablespoons packed brown sugar
- 2 teaspoons pepper
- ¾ teaspoon cayenne pepper

Combine all ingredients in bowl.

HERBES DE PROVENCE

Makes ½ cup

This delicate, aromatic blend of dried herbs from southern France can freshen up all kinds of foods. The mix makes for a delicious crust on Pan-Seared Flank Steak (page 195): Sprinkle it on after patting the steaks dry.

- **2 tablespoons dried thyme**
- **2 tablespoons dried marjoram**
- **2 tablespoons dried rosemary**
- **2 teaspoons fennel seeds**

Combine all ingredients in bowl.

FIVE-SPICE POWDER

Makes ½ cup

Chinese five-spice powder has a kick that offsets the richness in both sweet and savory recipes. In traditional Chinese cooking, the five elements of the cosmos—earth, fire, metal, water, and wood—are represented by five-spice powder. To add this rub to Oven-Roasted Salmon (page 197), sprinkle it on after rubbing the salmon with oil in step 1.

- **5 teaspoons fennel seeds**
- **4 teaspoons white peppercorns or 8 teaspoons Sichuan peppercorns**
- **1 tablespoon whole cloves**
- **8 star anise pods**
- **1 (3-inch) cinnamon stick, broken into pieces**

Process fennel seeds, peppercorns, and cloves in spice grinder until finely ground, about 30 seconds; transfer to small bowl. Process star anise and cinnamon in now-empty spice grinder until finely ground, about 30 seconds; transfer to bowl with other spices and stir to combine.

vegetables

While raw vegetables are nice, adding a cooked vegetable or two to a bowl introduces savory flavor as well as appealing contrasts in texture (and temperature if you add the vegetables warm). Even the simplest of seasonings on your vegetables—garlic, citrus, herbs—will bring layers of complexity to the finished bowl. Having one or two premade vegetables on hand makes assembling your bowl that much faster, but most of these can also be cooked at the last minute.

PAN-ROASTED ASPARAGUS

Makes 1½ cups, enough for 4 bowls

Quick-cooking pan-roasted asparagus spears combine the best of both worlds—browned exteriors with tender interiors. This recipe works best with asparagus that is at least ½ inch thick near the base. Do not use pencil-thin asparagus; it will overcook. You will need a 12-inch skillet with a tight-fitting lid for this recipe. The recipe can be easily doubled.

- 1 pound thick asparagus, trimmed
- 1 teaspoon extra-virgin olive oil or vegetable oil
- ½ teaspoon water

1. Trim bottom inch of asparagus spears and discard. Peel bottom halves of spears until white flesh is exposed. Heat oil in 12-inch nonstick skillet over medium-high heat until shimmering. Add half of asparagus with tips pointed in 1 direction and remaining asparagus with tips pointed in opposite direction. Shake skillet gently to help distribute spears evenly (they will not quite fit in single layer). Add water, cover, and cook until asparagus is bright green but still crisp, about 5 minutes.

2. Uncover, season with salt and pepper to taste, increase heat to high, and cook until asparagus is well browned on one side and tip of paring knife inserted at base of largest spear meets little resistance, 5 to 7 minutes. Cut asparagus as desired and season with salt and pepper to taste. (Asparagus can be refrigerated for up to 2 days.)

ROASTED BEETS

Makes 3 cups, enough for 4 bowls

Beets lend earthy flavor and bright color to a bowl, but with raw beets that color can also "bleed," creating an unattractive mess. Luckily, we found that roasting the beets in aluminum foil packets helped to concentrate their flavor and also minimized the amount of bleeding of their bright color into other bowl ingredients. The distinctively earthy-sweet flavor of the roasted beets, along with their vibrant purple-red color, made them an ideal component in our Rainbow Bowl (page 53), but you can also use these beets in a variety of other salad and grain bowls. The recipe can be easily doubled.

- 1 pound beets, trimmed

1. Adjust an oven rack to middle position and heat oven to 400 degrees. Wrap beets individually in aluminum foil and place on rimmed baking sheet. Roast until beets can be easily pierced with paring knife, 45 minutes to 1 hour, removing beets individually from oven as they finish cooking.

2. Open foil packets to allow steam to escape and let cool slightly. Once beets are cool enough to handle, rub off the skins using paper towels. Slice or chop beets as desired and season with salt and pepper to taste. (Beets can be refrigerated for up to 1 week.)

SAUTÉED BROCCOLI WITH GARLIC AND THYME

Makes 1½ cups, enough for 4 bowls

This crisp-tender broccoli with a lightly browned exterior quickly enhances the flavor of any bowl. You will need a 12-inch skillet with a tight-fitting lid for this recipe. Using broccoli florets, rather than a bunch of broccoli, can save valuable prep time.

- 1½ tablespoons extra-virgin olive oil or vegetable oil, divided
- 8 ounces broccoli florets, cut into 1-inch pieces
- ⅛ teaspoon table salt
- 1½ tablespoons water
- 1 garlic clove, minced
- ¼ teaspoon minced fresh thyme or pinch dried

1. Heat 1 tablespoon oil in 12-inch skillet over medium-high heat until just smoking. Add broccoli and salt and cook, without stirring, until beginning to brown, about 2 minutes. Add water, cover, and cook until broccoli is bright green but still crisp, about 2 minutes. Uncover and continue to cook until water has evaporated and broccoli is crisp-tender, about 2 minutes.

2. Clear center of pan, add remaining 1½ teaspoons oil, garlic, and thyme and cook, mashing garlic into skillet, until fragrant, about 30 seconds. Stir garlic mixture into broccoli. Transfer broccoli to bowl and season with salt and pepper to taste. (Broccoli can be refrigerated for up to 2 days.)

VARIATION
Sautéed Broccoli with Sesame Oil and Ginger

Substitute 1 tablespoon vegetable oil for olive oil when cooking broccoli in step 1. In garlic mixture, substitute 1 teaspoon toasted sesame oil for olive oil and add 1 teaspoon grated fresh ginger. Omit thyme.

ROASTED BUTTERNUT SQUASH

Makes 2 cups, enough for 4 bowls

Roasting butternut squash brings out its natural sweetness, making for a spectacularly autumnal bowl element. Cutting the squash into small, evenly sized pieces ensures that all of the squash cooks and browns at the same rate. The caramelized sweetness of roasted squash is the perfect counterpoint to bitter radicchio and tangy blue cheese in our Italian Harvest Bowl (page 75). This recipe can be easily doubled.

- 2 pounds butternut squash, peeled, seeded, and cut into ½-inch pieces (7 cups)
- 1 tablespoon extra-virgin olive oil or vegetable oil
- ½ teaspoon table salt
- ¼ teaspoon pepper

Adjust oven rack to lowest position and heat oven to 450 degrees. Line rimmed baking sheet with aluminum foil. Toss squash with oil, salt, and pepper and spread in even layer on prepared sheet. Roast until well browned and tender, 30 to 35 minutes, stirring once halfway through cooking. (Squash can be refrigerated for up to 1 week.)

Clockwise from Top Left: Sautéed Cherry Tomatoes (page 205), Sautéed Broccoli with Garlic and Thyme (page 203), Roasted Cauliflower (page 205), Roasted Carrots (page 205), Roasted Beets (page 202)

ROASTED CARROTS

Makes 2 cups, enough for 4 bowls

Carrots have a naturally sweet flavor that intensifies after roasting, making for a bowl topping that's as delicious as it is nutritious. This recipe can be easily doubled.

- 1½ pounds carrots, peeled and halved lengthwise
- 2 tablespoons extra-virgin olive oil, vegetable oil, or melted unsalted butter
- ½ teaspoon table salt
- ¼ teaspoon pepper

1. Adjust oven rack to lowest position and heat oven to 450 degrees. Toss carrots, oil, salt, and pepper together in bowl.

2. Spread in even layer on rimmed baking sheet, cut sides down. Roast until tender and cut sides are well browned, 15 to 25 minutes. Cut carrots as desired and season with salt and pepper to taste. (Carrots can be refrigerated for up to 2 days.)

SAUTÉED CHERRY TOMATOES

Makes 1½ cups, enough for 4 bowls

Sautéing highlights the tomatoes' sweetness, but if your tomatoes are especially sweet, you may want to reduce or omit the sugar. Grape tomatoes can be substituted. This recipe can be easily doubled.

- 1 teaspoon extra-virgin olive oil or vegetable oil
- 12 ounces cherry tomatoes, halved
- 1 teaspoon sugar
- 1 small garlic clove, minced
- 1 tablespoon chopped fresh basil

Heat oil in 12-inch nonstick skillet over medium-high heat until just smoking. Add tomatoes and sugar and cook, tossing often, until tomatoes begin to soften, about 1 minute. Stir in garlic and cook until fragrant, about 30 seconds. Transfer tomatoes to bowl, stir in basil, and season with salt and pepper to taste. (Cherry tomatoes can be refrigerated for up to 2 days.)

ROASTED CAULIFLOWER

Makes 2 cups, enough for 4 bowls

Cooking the cauliflower in large wedges achieves great browning, but you'll need to chop the cauliflower into pieces after roasting to make for easier eating in a bowl. This recipe can be easily doubled; adjust uncovered cooking time in steps 2 and 3 to 8 to 12 minutes.

- ½ head cauliflower (1 pound)
- 2 tablespoons extra-virgin olive oil or vegetable oil, divided
- ¼ teaspoon table salt, divided
- ⅛ teaspoon pepper, divided

1. Adjust oven rack to lowest position and heat oven to 475 degrees. Trim outer leaves off cauliflower and cut stem flush with bottom. Cut half head into 4 equal wedges. Place wedges, with either cut side down, on aluminum foil–lined rimmed baking sheet. Drizzle with 1 tablespoon oil and sprinkle with ⅛ teaspoon salt and pinch pepper. Gently rub oil and seasonings into cauliflower. Gently flip cauliflower and repeat on second cut side with remaining 1 tablespoon oil, remaining ⅛ teaspoon salt, and remaining pinch pepper.

2. Cover baking sheet tightly with foil and cook for 10 minutes. Remove foil and continue to roast until bottoms of cauliflower wedges are golden, 4 to 6 minutes.

3. Remove baking sheet from oven, use spatula to carefully flip wedges so other cut side is down, and continue to roast until cauliflower is golden all over, 4 to 6 minutes. Cut cauliflower as desired and season with salt and pepper to taste. (Cauliflower can be refrigerated for up to 2 days.)

VARIATION
Spicy Roasted Cauliflower

Sprinkle cauliflower with 1 teaspoon chili powder in step 1.

foil–lined rimmed baking sheet, and lightly brush both sides with 1½ teaspoons oil. Broil eggplant until mahogany brown and lightly charred, 4 to 8 minutes per side.

3. Whisk remaining 1½ tablespoons oil, vinegar, capers, garlic, lemon zest, oregano, and pepper together in large bowl. Add eggplant and mint and gently toss to combine.

4. Let eggplant cool to room temperature, about 1 hour. Cut eggplant as desired and season with salt and pepper to taste. (Eggplant can be refrigerated for up to 2 days.)

MARINATED EGGPLANT WITH CAPERS AND MINT

Makes 1½ cups, enough for 4 bowls

This bold component boasts briny, herby, earthy, bright flavors. We prefer kosher salt because residual grains wipe away easily; if using table salt, reduce all salt amounts by half. This recipe can be easily doubled. Cooking times will vary depending on the broiler; watch the eggplant carefully.

- 12 ounces Italian eggplant, sliced into 1-inch-thick rounds
- ½ teaspoon kosher salt
- 2 tablespoons extra-virgin olive oil or vegetable oil, divided
- 2 teaspoons red wine vinegar
- 1 teaspoon capers, rinsed and minced
- 1 small garlic clove, minced
- ¼ teaspoon grated lemon zest
- ¼ teaspoon minced fresh oregano
- ⅛ teaspoon pepper
- 1 tablespoon minced fresh mint

1. Spread eggplant on paper towel–lined baking sheet, sprinkle both sides with salt, and let sit for 30 minutes.

2. Adjust oven rack 4 inches from broiler element and heat broiler. Thoroughly pat eggplant dry with paper towels, arrange in single layer on aluminum

SIMPLE SAUTÉED GREEN BEANS WITH GARLIC

Makes 1½ cups, enough for 4 bowls

A quick sauté turns green beans into a perfectly crisp-tender bowl component. You will need a 12-inch nonstick skillet with a tight-fitting lid for this recipe. The recipe can be easily doubled.

- ½ teaspoon extra-virgin olive oil or vegetable oil
- 8 ounces green beans, trimmed and halved crosswise
  Pinch table salt
- 2 tablespoons water
- 1 garlic clove, minced

1. Heat oil in 12-inch nonstick skillet over medium heat until just smoking. Add green beans and salt and cook, stirring occasionally, until spotty brown, 4 to 6 minutes.

2. Add water, cover, and cook until green beans are bright green but still crisp, about 2 minutes. Uncover, increase heat to high, and cook until water evaporates, 30 to 60 seconds.

3. Stir in garlic and cook until green beans are crisp-tender, lightly browned, and beginning to wrinkle, 1 to 3 minutes. Season with salt and pepper to taste. (Green beans can be refrigerated for up to 2 days.)

SAUTÉED MUSHROOMS WITH SHALLOTS AND THYME

Makes 1½ cups, enough for 4 bowls

Umami-packed mushrooms can take any bowl over the top. Use a single type of mushroom or a combination, but yields will vary. Stem and halve portobellos and cut each half crosswise into ½-inch pieces. Trim white or cremini mushrooms; quarter if large or medium, and halve if small. Tear trimmed oyster mushrooms into 1- to 1½-inch pieces. Stem shiitake mushrooms; quarter large caps and halve small caps. You can substitute white wine for the Marsala.

- 10 ounces mushrooms
- 2 tablespoons water
- ¼ teaspoon extra-virgin olive oil or vegetable oil
- ½ tablespoon unsalted butter
- 1 small shallot, minced
- 1½ teaspoons minced fresh thyme or ½ teaspoon dried
- ⅛ teaspoon table salt
- ⅛ teaspoon pepper
- 2 tablespoons dry Marsala
- ¼ cup chicken or vegetable broth

1. Cook mushrooms and water in 12-inch nonstick skillet over high heat, stirring occasionally, until skillet is almost dry and mushrooms begin to sizzle, 4 to 8 minutes. Reduce heat to medium-high. Add oil and toss until mushrooms are evenly coated. Continue to cook, stirring occasionally, until mushrooms are well browned, 4 to 8 minutes longer.

2. Reduce heat to medium. Push mushrooms to sides of skillet. Add butter to center. When butter has melted, add shallot, thyme, salt, and pepper and cook, stirring constantly, until fragrant, about 30 seconds. Stir in mushrooms, then add Marsala and cook until liquid has evaporated, 2 to 3 minutes. Stir in broth and cook until glaze is reduced by half, about 3 minutes. Season with salt and pepper to taste. (Mushrooms can be refrigerated for up to 2 days.)

VARIATION

Sautéed Mushrooms with Sesame and Ginger

Substitute 1½ teaspoons vegetable oil for butter and 1 tablespoon mirin and 1 tablespoon soy sauce for Marsala. Omit shallot and thyme. After browning mushrooms in step 1, stir in 1½ teaspoons toasted sesame seeds and 1½ teaspoons grated fresh ginger and cook until fragrant, about 30 seconds. Stir in ½ teaspoon toasted sesame oil and sprinkle with 1 thinly sliced scallion after seasoning with salt and pepper to taste in step 2.

ROASTED BELL PEPPERS

Makes 1½ cups, enough for 4 bowls

Perfect roasted peppers are easy to do at home. Cooking times will vary depending on broiler and thickness of bell pepper walls; watch carefully as the peppers cook. Use any color peppers, but note that green bell peppers retain some bitterness when roasted.

- 3 large bell peppers

1. Adjust oven rack 4 inches from broiler element and heat broiler. Line rimmed baking sheet with aluminum foil and spray with vegetable oil spray. Slice ½ inch from top and bottom of each bell pepper. Gently remove stems from tops. Twist and pull out each core, using knife to loosen if necessary. Cut slit down 1 side of each bell pepper.

2. Turn each bell pepper skin side down and gently press so it opens to create long strip. Slide knife along insides of bell peppers to remove remaining ribs and seeds.

3. Arrange bell pepper strips, tops, and bottoms skin side up on prepared sheet and flatten all pieces with your hand. Broil until skin is puffed and most of surface is well charred, 10 to 13 minutes, rotating sheet halfway through broiling.

4. Using tongs, pile bell peppers in center of foil. Gather foil over bell peppers and crimp to form pouch. Let steam for 10 minutes. Open foil packet carefully and spread out bell peppers. When cool enough to handle, peel bell peppers and discard skins. Cut peppers as desired. (Bell peppers can be refrigerated for up to 2 days.)

SAUTÉED RADISHES

Makes 2 cups, enough for 4 bowls

Although we often leave radishes raw for crunch since their crisp texture can be a great addition to a bowl, they also have a hidden softer side that we love. Roasting quartered radishes softens their exteriors and helps to develop their earthiness, adding deeper flavor when used as a bowl topping, as in our Forbidden Rice Bowl with Salmon (page 70). This recipe can be easily doubled.

  1 tablespoon unsalted butter, cut into 3 pieces
 12 ounces radishes, trimmed and quartered
 ⅛ teaspoon table salt
   Pinch pepper
  1 small garlic clove, minced

Melt butter in 12-inch skillet over medium-high heat. Add radishes, salt, and pepper and cook, stirring occasionally, until radishes are lightly browned and crisp-tender, 10 to 12 minutes. Stir in garlic and cook until fragrant, about 30 seconds. Season with salt and pepper to taste. (Radishes can be refrigerated for up to 2 days.)

VARIATIONS
Sautéed Radishes with Chili
Stir ½ teaspoon paprika and ¼ teaspoon chili powder into radishes with garlic.

Sautéed Radishes with Vadouvan Curry and Almonds
We prefer the flavor of vadouvan curry here, but any variety will work.

   Substitute ¾ teaspoon vadouvan curry for garlic. Sprinkle radishes with 2 tablespoons coarsely chopped toasted almonds before serving.

SNAP PEAS WITH LEMON, GARLIC, AND BASIL

Makes 1½ cups, enough for 4 bowls

Lightly crisp snap peas add both flavor and crunch to any bowl. Feel free to substitute other fresh herbs, such as parsley, chives, cilantro, tarragon, or savory, for the basil. You will need a 12-inch nonstick skillet with a tight-fitting lid for this recipe. The recipe can be easily doubled.

  1 teaspoon extra-virgin olive oil or vegetable oil, divided
  8 ounces snap peas, trimmed
  2 tablespoons water
 ⅛ teaspoon table salt
  1 small garlic clove, minced
  1 teaspoon lemon juice
  1 teaspoon chopped fresh basil

1. Heat ½ teaspoon oil in 12-inch nonstick skillet over medium-high heat until shimmering. Add snap peas and cook until lightly browned, about 2 minutes. Add water and salt, cover, and cook until snap peas are bright green and beginning to soften, 1 to 2 minutes.

2. Uncover and cook until water is evaporated, about 30 seconds. Clear center of skillet and add remaining ½ teaspoon oil and garlic. Cook, mashing garlic into pan, until fragrant, about 30 seconds. Stir snap peas into garlic. Transfer snap peas to bowl, stir in lemon juice and basil, and season with salt and pepper to taste. (Snap peas can be refrigerated for up to 2 days.)

VARIATION
Sesame Snap Peas
Add 1½ teaspoons soy sauce, 1 teaspoon sugar, and ½ teaspoon rice vinegar with garlic. Omit lemon juice and basil. Instead, toss snap peas with 1 teaspoon toasted sesame seeds and ⅛ teaspoon toasted sesame oil before serving.

2. Flip squash over and let cool slightly. Holding squash with clean dish towel over large bowl, use fork to scrape squash flesh from skin while shredding it into fine pieces.

3. Drain excess liquid from bowl, then gently stir in Parmesan, basil, lemon juice, and remaining 1½ teaspoons oil. Season with salt and pepper to taste. (Squash can be refrigerated for up to 2 days.)

VARIATION
Spaghetti Squash with Asian Flavors
Omit Parmesan, basil, lemon juice, and remaining 1½ teaspoons oil in step 3. Toss roasted shredded squash with 1 thinly sliced scallion, 1½ teaspoons soy sauce, 1¼ teaspoons vegetable oil, ½ teaspoon rice vinegar, ¼ teaspoon toasted sesame oil, and ¼ teaspoon toasted sesame seeds before serving.

SPAGHETTI SQUASH WITH BASIL AND PARMESAN
Makes 2 cups, enough for 4 bowls as a topping
When roasted, spaghetti squash transforms into noodle-like strands that work equally well as a bowl topping or base. Choose a firm squash with an even, pale-yellow color. Avoid greenish-tinged squashes, which are immature, and those that yield to gentle pressure, which are old. This recipe can be easily doubled; use a 13 by 9-inch baking dish instead of an 8-inch baking dish.

- ½ **spaghetti squash (1¼ pounds), halved lengthwise and seeded**
- 1 **tablespoon extra-virgin olive oil or vegetable oil, divided**
- ⅛ **teaspoon table salt**
- ⅛ **teaspoon pepper**
- 2 **tablespoons grated Parmesan cheese**
- 1 **teaspoon chopped fresh basil**
- ½ **teaspoon lemon juice**

1. Adjust oven rack to middle position and heat oven to 450 degrees. Brush cut sides of squash with 1½ teaspoons of the oil and sprinkle with salt and pepper. Lay squash cut sides down in 8-inch baking dish. Roast squash until just tender and tip of paring knife can be slipped into flesh with slight resistance, 25 to 30 minutes.

ROASTED SWEET POTATOES
Makes 2 cups, enough for 4 bowls
Earthy sweet potatoes are so hearty that you can use them in place of meat to bulk your bowl up, making for a delicious, and vegetarian, meal—as in our Harvest Bowl (page 20). Choose potatoes that are as even in width as possible; trimming the small ends prevents them from burning. We like the texture that unpeeled potatoes add to our bowls; just be sure to scrub them well before prepping. Or you can peel the potatoes if you prefer.

- 1 **pound sweet potatoes, halved lengthwise then sliced crosswise ¼ inch thick**
- 1 **tablespoon extra-virgin olive oil or vegetable oil**
- ¼ **teaspoon table salt**

Adjust oven rack to middle position and heat oven to 400 degrees. Toss potatoes, oil, and salt together in bowl, then spread in even layer on rimmed baking sheet. Roast until potatoes are beginning to brown, 15 to 20 minutes, flipping slices halfway through roasting. Let potatoes cool for 5 minutes then season with salt and pepper to taste. (Sweet potatoes can be refrigerated for up to 2 days.)

toppings

Toppings are the crispy, crunchy, salty, savory additions that can take any bowl from average to amazing. Think about these recipes as your secret weapon against uninspired bowls; many can last in your pantry for over a week so you can turn to them again and again without having to make a fresh batch each time.

QUICK TOASTED NUTS

Makes 2 cups

Nuts are an easy way to add hearty crunch to your bowl, and toasting them helps to bring out their flavorful oils. This method can be used with a variety of nuts and seasonings to adapt to any bowl flavors.

- 1 tablespoon extra-virgin olive oil or vegetable oil
- 2 cups skin-on raw whole almonds, shelled walnuts, or shelled pistachios
- 1 teaspoon table salt
- ¼ teaspoon pepper

Heat oil in 12-inch nonstick skillet over medium-high heat until just shimmering. Add nuts, salt, and pepper and reduce heat to medium-low. Cook, stirring often, until nuts are fragrant and their color deepens slightly, about 8 minutes. Transfer nuts to paper towel–lined plate and let cool. (Nuts can be stored in airtight container at room temperature for up to 5 days.)

VARIATIONS
Rosemary Nuts

Add ½ teaspoon dried rosemary to skillet with nuts.

Orange-Fennel Nuts

Add 1 teaspoon grated orange zest and ½ teaspoon ground fennel seeds to skillet with nuts.

Spiced Nuts

Add 2 teaspoons grated lemon zest, 1 teaspoon ground coriander seeds, and ½ teaspoon hot paprika to skillet with nuts.

Lemon-Garlic Nuts

Add ½ teaspoon grated lemon zest and 1 minced garlic clove to skillet with nuts. Just before serving, toss with another ½ teaspoon grated lemon zest.

SPICED PEPITAS OR SUNFLOWER SEEDS

Makes ½ cup

Salty, crunchy, spicy seeds are an easy topping that elevates a basic bowl in a snap.

- 2 teaspoons extra-virgin olive oil or vegetable oil
- ½ cup pepitas or sunflower seeds
- ½ teaspoon paprika
- ½ teaspoon coriander
- ¼ teaspoon table salt

Heat oil in 12-inch skillet over medium heat until shimmering. Add pepitas, paprika, coriander, and salt. Cook, stirring constantly, until seeds are toasted, about 2 minutes; transfer to bowl and let cool. (Seeds can be stored in airtight container at room temperature for up to 5 days.)

1. Adjust oven rack to upper-middle position and heat oven to 300 degrees. Line 8-inch square baking pan with parchment paper and spray parchment with vegetable oil spray. Whisk maple syrup, egg white, oil, soy sauce, caraway seeds, salt, and pepper together in large bowl. Stir in oats, sunflower seeds, pepitas, sesame seeds, and nigella seeds until well combined.

2. Transfer oat mixture to prepared pan and spread into even layer. Using stiff metal spatula, press oat mixture until very compact. Bake until golden brown and fragrant, 45 to 55 minutes, rotating pan halfway through baking.

3. Transfer pan to wire rack and let brittle cool completely, about 1 hour. Break cooled brittle into pieces of desired size, discarding parchment. (Brittle can be stored in airtight container at room temperature for up to 1 month.)

SAVORY SEED BRITTLE

Makes 2 cups

For a topping that can instantly take any bowl to the next level, we developed a seed brittle packed with both outstanding texture and delicious savory flavor. To achieve the ideal crunchy, brittle texture that would break into bite-size pieces, we added an egg white and some maple syrup, which also added just a bit of sweetness to offset all the savory flavors. This brittle can last up to 1 month, making it perfect to keep on hand as an easy bowl upgrade, as in our Harvest Bowl (page 20) and Creamy Butternut Squash Soup with Apples and Pork (page 162). Do not substitute quick or instant oats in this recipe.

 2 tablespoons maple syrup
 1 large egg white
 1 tablespoon extra-virgin olive oil or vegetable oil
 1 tablespoon soy sauce
 1 tablespoon caraway seeds, crushed
 ½ teaspoon table salt
 ¼ teaspoon pepper
 ½ cup old-fashioned rolled oats
 ⅓ cup sunflower seeds
 ⅓ cup pepitas
 2 tablespoons sesame seeds
 2 tablespoons nigella seeds

PISTACHIO DUKKAH

Makes ½ cup

This Middle Eastern spice blend adds a powerful boost of flavor when sprinkled on soup, grain, or bean bowls. If you do not own a spice grinder, you can process the spices in a mini food processor.

 1½ teaspoons coriander seeds, toasted
 ¾ teaspoon cumin seeds, toasted
 ½ teaspoon fennel seeds, toasted
 2 tablespoons sesame seeds, toasted
 3 tablespoons shelled pistachios, toasted and chopped fine
 ½ teaspoon flake sea salt, such as Maldon
 ½ teaspoon pepper

Process coriander seeds, cumin seeds, and fennel seeds in spice grinder until finely ground, about 30 seconds. Add sesame seeds and pulse until coarsely ground, about 4 pulses; transfer to small bowl. Stir in pistachios, salt, and pepper. (Dukkah can be refrigerated for up to 3 months.)

CRISPY CHICKPEAS

Makes 1²/₃ cups

For a crunchy protein boost, crispy chickpeas add outstanding texture, and their versatile flavor means they can take on a variety of different spice combinations. This recipe calls for a metal baking pan; using glass or ceramic will result in unevenly cooked chickpeas.

  2 (15-ounce) cans chickpeas
  3 tablespoons extra-virgin olive oil or vegetable oil
 ⅛ teaspoon table salt
     Pinch cayenne pepper

1. Adjust oven rack to middle position and heat oven to 350 degrees. Place chickpeas in colander and let drain for 10 minutes. Line large plate with double layer of paper towels. Spread chickpeas over plate in even layer. Microwave until exteriors of chickpeas are dry and many have split slightly at seams, 8 to 12 minutes.

2. Transfer chickpeas to 13 by 9-inch metal baking pan. Add oil and stir until evenly coated. Using spatula, spread chickpeas into single layer. Transfer to oven and roast for 30 minutes. While chickpeas are roasting, combine salt and cayenne in small bowl.

3. Stir chickpeas and crowd toward center of pan, avoiding edges of pan as much as possible. Continue to roast until chickpeas appear dry, slightly shriveled, and deep golden brown, 20 to 40 minutes longer. (To test for doneness, remove a few paler chickpeas and let cool briefly before tasting; if interiors are soft, return to oven for 5 minutes before testing again.)

4. Transfer chickpeas to large bowl and toss with spice mixture to coat. Season with salt to taste and let cool completely. (Chickpeas can be stored in airtight container at room temperature for up to 1 week.)

VARIATIONS
Indian-Spiced Crispy Chickpeas

Increase cayenne to ⅛ teaspoon. Add 2 teaspoons paprika, 1 teaspoon ground coriander, ½ teaspoon ground turmeric, ½ teaspoon ground allspice, ½ teaspoon ground cumin, and ½ teaspoon sugar to bowl with salt and cayenne.

Barbecue-Spiced Crispy Chickpeas

Increase cayenne to ⅛ teaspoon. Add 1 tablespoon smoked paprika, 1½ teaspoons sugar, 1 teaspoon garlic powder, and ½ teaspoon onion powder to bowl with salt and cayenne.

Spanish-Spiced Crispy Chickpeas

Increase cayenne to ⅛ teaspoon. Add 1 tablespoon smoked paprika, ½ teaspoon ground coriander, and ¼ teaspoon ground cumin to bowl with salt and cayenne.

CRISPY SHALLOTS

Makes ½ cup

Crispy shallots are one of our favorite bowl toppings to add a quick boost of texture and oniony flavor. To make the preparation as simple as possible, we turned to the microwave to create shallots with a fried exterior with minimal cleanup.

  3 shallots, sliced thin
 ½ cup vegetable oil, for frying

Microwave shallots and oil in medium bowl for 5 minutes. Stir shallots, then microwave for 2 more minutes. Repeat stirring and microwaving in 2-minute increments until beginning to brown, then repeat stirring and microwaving in 30-second increments until deep golden brown. Using slotted spoon, transfer shallots to paper towel–lined plate and season with salt to taste. Let drain and crisp for about 5 minutes. (Shallots can be stored in airtight container at room temperature for up to 1 month.)

Top to Bottom: Crispy Tortilla Strips (page 215), Orange-Fennel Nuts (page 210), Vegan Parmesan Substitute (page 215), Spanish-Spiced Crispy Chickpeas (page 212), Crispy Rice Noodles (page 215)

GARLIC CHIPS

Makes ½ cup

Sliced garlic takes just a few minutes to crisp up in the pan. The results are crispy chips that will add a welcomed flavor boost to a variety of bowls.

  3 tablespoons vegetable oil, for frying
  8 garlic cloves, sliced thin

Heat oil and garlic in medium saucepan over medium heat, stirring constantly once garlic starts to sizzle. Cook until garlic is light golden brown, 3 to 5 minutes. Using slotted spoon, transfer garlic to paper towel–lined plate and season with salt to taste. (Garlic chips can be stored in airtight container at room temperature for up to 3 days.)

PITA CRUMBLE

Makes 2 cups

We use this crisp, toasty pita topping to add delicious crunch to our Mediterranean-inspired bowls.

  1 (8-inch) pita bread
  4 teaspoons extra-virgin olive oil or vegetable oil
  ⅛ teaspoon table salt
  ⅛ teaspoon pepper

Adjust oven rack to middle position and heat oven to 375 degrees. Using kitchen shears, cut around perimeter of pita and separate into 2 thin rounds. Cut each round in half. Place pitas smooth side down on wire rack set in rimmed baking sheet. Brush surface of pitas with oil then sprinkle with salt and pepper. Bake until pitas are crisp and pale golden, 10 to 14 minutes. Let cool to room temperature, then crumble into bite-size pieces. (Pita crumble can be stored in airtight container at room temperature for up to 3 days.)

FRICO CRUMBLE

Makes 1½ cups

This thin, crispy, crumbly topping adds a blast of cheesy flavor to noodle bowls like our Creamy Corn Bucatini Bowl (page 140) and to creamy, hearty bowls like our Polenta Bowl with Broccoli Rabe and Fried Eggs (page 101). We prefer aged Asiago for our frico, but aged Manchego or cheddar cheese are also good options. Use a Microplane to grate the cheese.

  4 ounces aged Asiago cheese, finely grated (2 cups), divided

1. Sprinkle half of cheese evenly over bottom of cold 10-inch nonstick skillet. Cook over medium heat until edges are lacy and light golden, 2 to 3 minutes. Remove skillet from heat and let sit for 1 minute.

2. Using 2 spatulas, carefully flip frico. Return to medium heat and cook until second side is golden, about 1 minute. Carefully slide frico to plate and set aside until cooled, about 10 minutes.

3. Wipe skillet clean with paper towels and repeat with remaining cheese. Let cool to room temperature, then crumble into bite-size pieces. (Frico can be stored in airtight container at room temperature for up to 5 days.)

VEGAN PARMESAN SUBSTITUTE

Makes about 1½ cups

For a vegan alternative to Parmesan cheese, a combination of cashews and savory nutritional yeast along with pine nuts and olives re-creates Parmesan's distinctive umami flavor.

- ¾ cup raw cashews
- 3 tablespoons nutritional yeast
- 2 tablespoons raw pine nuts
- 1 tablespoon chopped green olives, patted dry
- ¾ teaspoon salt

1. Adjust oven rack to middle position and heat oven to 275 degrees. Process all ingredients in food processor until finely ground, about 1 minute, scraping down sides of bowl as needed.

2. Spread mixture on rimmed baking sheet in even layer. Bake until mixture is light golden and dry to the touch, about 20 minutes, stirring mixture and rotating pan halfway through baking.

3. Let cool to room temperature then break apart any large clumps. (Parmesan substitute can be refrigerated for up to 1 month.)

CRISPY TORTILLA STRIPS

Makes 2 cups

For crunchy tortilla strips that add texture to our bowls we turned to the oven instead of frying.

- 8 (6-inch) corn tortillas, cut into ½-inch-wide strips
- 1 tablespoon extra-virgin olive oil or vegetable oil

Adjust oven rack to middle position and heat oven to 425 degrees. Toss tortilla strips with oil, spread on rimmed baking sheet, and bake, stirring frequently, until deep golden brown and crisp, 8 to 12 minutes. Transfer to paper towel–lined plate and season with salt to taste. (Tortilla strips can be stored in airtight container at room temperature for up to 1 week.)

CROUTONS

Makes 1½ cups

The flavor and crunch of homemade buttery croutons is unbeatable on salad and soup bowls.

- 3 tablespoons unsalted butter
- 1 tablespoon extra-virgin olive oil or vegetable oil
- 2 slices hearty white sandwich bread, cut into ½-inch pieces (1½ cups)

Heat butter and oil in 10-inch skillet over medium heat until butter melts. Add bread pieces and cook, stirring frequently, until golden brown, about 10 minutes. Transfer croutons to paper towel–lined plate and season with salt to taste. (Croutons can be stored in airtight container at room temperature for up to 1 week.)

VARIATIONS
Garlic Croutons

Add 1 minced garlic clove to skillet with butter and oil.

Buttery Rye Croutons

Substitute rye bread for white sandwich bread.

CRISPY RICE NOODLES

Makes 8 cups

These light, airy, crispy fried rice noodles are as beautiful a topping as they are delicious. The noodles will expand very quickly in the oil, so be sure to prepare the paper towel–lined sheet before frying.

- 6 cups vegetable oil, for frying
- 2 ounces rice vermicelli noodles

Set wire rack in rimmed baking sheet and line with triple layer of paper towels. Heat oil in large saucepan over medium-high heat to 400 degrees. Add noodles then immediately turn off heat. Fry until noodles puff and turn bright white, 10 to 30 seconds. Using wire skimmer, tongs, or slotted spoon, remove noodles from oil, transfer to prepared sheet to drain, and let cool completely. (Rice noodles can be stored in airtight container at room temperature for up to 1 month.)

quick pickles

Pickles can add bright flavor, crunch, and color to any grain bowl, but making them yourself is typically a chore; enter quick pickles. While they don't last as long as truly fermented pickles, they achieve similar flavors and textures in a flash.

QUICK PICKLED GRAPES

Makes 1⅓ cups

Pickling adds vibrantly acidic flavor to grapes, rendering a perfect sweet-tart combination.

- ⅓ cup white wine vinegar
- 1 tablespoon sugar
- ½ teaspoon table salt
- 8 ounces seedless grapes, halved

Microwave vinegar, sugar, and salt in medium bowl until simmering, 1 to 2 minutes. Stir in grapes and let sit, stirring occasionally, for 45 minutes. Drain. (Drained pickled grapes can be refrigerated for up to 1 week.)

QUICK PICKLED FENNEL

Makes 2 cups

These quick pickles offer a crunchy burst of sweet anise and fresh citrus flavors to any bowl.

- ¾ cup seasoned rice vinegar
- ¼ cup water
- 1 (1-inch) strip orange zest
- 1 garlic clove, peeled and halved
- ¼ teaspoon fennel seeds
- ⅛ teaspoon black peppercorns
- ⅛ teaspoon yellow mustard seeds
- 1 fennel bulb, stalks discarded, bulb halved, cored, and sliced thin

Combine vinegar, water, orange zest, garlic, fennel seeds, peppercorns, and mustard seeds in 4-cup liquid measuring cup. Microwave until boiling, about 3 minutes. Stir in fennel until completely submerged and let cool completely, about 30 minutes. Drain. (Drained pickled fennel can be refrigerated for up to 6 weeks; fennel will soften significantly after 6 weeks.)

QUICK SWEET AND SPICY PICKLED RED ONIONS

Makes 1 cup

Jalapeños, red wine vinegar, and a little sugar turn simple red onions into a flavor-packed topping that enlivens your bowl with sweet and spicy flavors.

- 2 jalapeño chiles, stemmed, seeded, and sliced into thin rings
- 1 cup red wine vinegar
- ⅓ cup sugar
- ⅛ teaspoon table salt
- 1 red onion, halved and sliced thin through root end

Microwave jalapeños, vinegar, sugar, and salt in medium bowl until simmering, 1 to 2 minutes. Stir in onion and let sit, stirring occasionally, for 45 minutes. Drain. (Drained pickled onions can be refrigerated for up to 1 week.)

QUICK PICKLED CARROT RIBBONS

Makes 1½ cups

For tart crunch, we love the flavor of pickled carrot ribbons as a bowl topping.

- 1 cup rice vinegar
- ⅓ cup sugar
- ½ teaspoon table salt
- ¼ teaspoon red pepper flakes
- 4 carrots, peeled and shaved into ribbons with vegetable peeler

Microwave vinegar, sugar, salt, and pepper flakes in medium bowl until simmering, 1 to 2 minutes. Stir in carrots and let sit, stirring occasionally, for 45 minutes. Drain. (Drained pickled carrots can be refrigerated for up to 1 week.)

Try one of these combinations, or use the ideas as inspiration. **Top:** Beet Noodles (page 193), Pan-Seared Tofu (page 198), Roasted Carrots (page 205), Crispy Shallots (page 212), Tahini-Yogurt Sauce (page 226) **Bottom Right:** Creamy Parmesan Polenta (page 192), Zhoug (page 223), Roasted Butternut Squash (page 203), Easy-Peel Soft-Cooked Egg (page 199), Pistachio Dukkah (page 211) **Bottom Left:** Farro (page 189), Sautéed Cherry Tomatoes (page 205), Quick Sweet and Spicy Pickled Red Onions (page 216), Pan-Seared Flank Steak (page 195), Ranch Dressing (page 223), basil

dressings & sauces

No bowl would be complete without a drizzle of sauce to add crucial moisture, flavor, and even color. Homemade dressings and sauces don't have to be intimidating. They're often made with pantry ingredients and can stay in your refrigerator for at least a few days to brighten up bowls throughout the week.

MAKE-AHEAD VINAIGRETTE

Makes 1 cup

We love a simple vinaigrette on many of our salad and grain bowls, but we wanted an easy version we could make ahead for packed lunches and week-night dinners that would stay emulsified in the fridge. We found that the right combination of emulsifiers (Dijon and mayonnaise) and a stabilizer (molasses) gave us a vinaigrette with the perfect balanced consistency, and as a bonus we could shake the dressing up in a jar rather than whisking. Regular or light mayonnaise can be used in this recipe. Do not use blackstrap molasses.

- 1 tablespoon mayonnaise
- 1 tablespoon molasses
- 1 tablespoon Dijon mustard
- ½ teaspoon table salt
- ¼ cup wine vinegar
- ½ cup extra-virgin olive oil, divided
- ¼ cup vegetable oil

1. Combine mayonnaise, molasses, mustard, and salt in 2-cup jar with tight-fitting lid. Stir until mixture is milky in appearance and no lumps of mayonnaise or molasses remain. Add vinegar, seal jar, and shake until smooth, about 10 seconds.

2. Add ¼ cup olive oil, seal jar, and shake vigorously until thoroughly combined, about 10 seconds. Repeat, adding remaining ¼ cup olive oil and vegetable oil in 2 additions, shaking vigorously until thoroughly combined after each addition. (Vinaigrette can be refrigerated for up to 1 week; shake to recombine before using.)

POMEGRANATE-HONEY VINAIGRETTE

Makes about 1 cup

This vinaigrette perfectly pairs sweet and tart. To avoid off-flavors, make sure to reduce the fruit juice in a nonreactive stainless-steel saucepan.

- 2 cups pomegranate juice
- 1 tablespoon honey
- 3 tablespoons red wine vinegar
- 2 tablespoons extra-virgin olive oil or vegetable oil
- 1 tablespoon minced shallot
- ½ teaspoon table salt
- ½ teaspoon pepper

Bring pomegranate juice and honey to boil in small saucepan over medium-high heat. Reduce to simmer and cook until thickened and juice measures about ⅔ cup, 15 to 20 minutes. Transfer syrup to medium bowl and refrigerate until cool, about 15 minutes. Whisk in vinegar, oil, shallot, salt, and pepper until combined. (Vinaigrette can be refrigerated for up to 1 week; whisk to recombine before using.)

VARIATIONS
Apple Cider–Sage Vinaigrette
Substitute apple cider for pomegranate juice, and cider vinegar for red wine vinegar. Add ½ teaspoon minced fresh sage to syrup with vinegar.

Orange-Ginger Vinaigrette
Substitute orange juice for pomegranate juice, and lime juice for red wine vinegar. Add 1 teaspoon grated fresh ginger to syrup with lime juice.

SESAME-SCALLION VINAIGRETTE

Makes ¾ cup

This simple, flavorful vinaigrette, which comes together in just seconds, is light enough to add subtle flavor, as in our Tofu Sushi Bowl (page 68). Just 1 teaspoon of chili oil packs in enough heat to elevate the potent combination of soy, mirin, sesame, and vinegar. For a milder sauce, omit the chili oil.

¼ cup soy sauce
2 tablespoons rice vinegar
2 tablespoons mirin
2 tablespoons water
1 teaspoon chili oil (optional)
½ teaspoon toasted sesame oil
1 scallion, minced

Whisk all ingredients together in bowl. (Vinaigrette can be refrigerated for up to 3 days; whisk to recombine before using.)

SRIRACHA-LIME VINAIGRETTE

Makes about 1 cup

This bright, spicy, fresh vinaigrette adds a burst of heat and citrus to salad or grain bowls. The sriracha in this dressing packs a punch, but the sweetness of honey, the bold flavor of fresh ginger, the umami of fish sauce, and the freshness of lime juice balance out the heat to make for a dressing that adds impressive flavor, as in our Sriracha-Lime Tofu Salad Bowl (page 19). For a vegetarian vinaigrette, use Bragg Liquid Aminos instead of fish sauce.

¼ cup lime juice (2 limes)
2 tablespoons honey
2 tablespoons fish sauce
1 tablespoon grated fresh ginger
1 tablespoon sriracha
⅓ cup extra-virgin olive oil

Whisk lime juice, honey, fish sauce, ginger, and sriracha together in medium bowl. While whisking constantly, slowly drizzle in oil until combined. (Vinaigrette can be refrigerated for up to 3 days; whisk to recombine before using.)

SESAME SAUCE

Makes ⅓ cup

The deep nutty flavor of toasted sesame seeds is the star of this sauce, which gets a deliciously creamy texture from mayonnaise and a balance of salty, sweet, and tangy flavors from a combination of miso, lemon juice, sugar, and garlic. This sauce works well drizzled over salads, grain bowls, and noodle bowls. We prefer the flavor of red miso here, but white miso can be substituted.

¼ cup sesame seeds, toasted
2 tablespoons mayonnaise
1 tablespoon red miso
2 teaspoons lemon juice
2 teaspoons sugar
1 garlic clove, minced
½ teaspoon water

Whisk all ingredients together in bowl. (Sauce can be refrigerated for up to 3 days.)

2. Process shallot mixture, sugar, and lime juice in food processor until thick paste forms, 15 to 30 seconds, scraping down sides of bowl as needed.

3. Return paste to now-empty saucepan and add fish sauce and 2 tablespoons reserved oil. Bring to simmer over medium-low heat. Cook, stirring frequently, until mixture is thickened and has jam-like consistency, 4 to 5 minutes. Off heat, season with extra lime juice, extra fish sauce, and salt to taste. (Jam can be refrigerated for up to 1 month.)

GOCHUJANG SAUCE
Makes ½ cup
Spicy Korean gochujang, which helps create this quick and flavorful sauce, is sold in Asian markets and many supermarkets. If you can't find it, substitute sriracha and omit the water.

- ¼ cup gochujang
- 3 tablespoons water
- 2 tablespoons toasted sesame oil
- 1 teaspoon sugar

Whisk all ingredients together in bowl. (Sauce can be refrigerated for up to 3 days.)

MISO-GINGER SAUCE
Makes about ¾ cup
For a thick, saucy dressing packed with flavor, we turned to miso and potent fresh ginger.

- ¼ cup mayonnaise
- 3 tablespoons red miso
- 2 tablespoons water
- 1 tablespoon maple syrup
- 1 tablespoon sesame oil
- 1½ teaspoons sherry vinegar
- 1½ teaspoons grated fresh ginger

Whisk all ingredients together in bowl. (Sauce can be refrigerated for up to 3 days.)

THAI CHILI JAM
Makes ¾ cup
This sweet, savory, spicy jam adds a kick of heat to noodle and soup bowls. Slice the shallots to a consistent thickness to ensure even cooking.

- ½ cup vegetable oil, for frying
- 2 large shallots, sliced thin
- 4 large garlic cloves, sliced thin
- 10 dried arbol chiles, stemmed, halved lengthwise, and seeds reserved
- 2 tablespoons packed brown sugar
- 3 tablespoons lime juice, plus extra for seasoning (2 limes)
- 2 tablespoons fish sauce, plus extra for seasoning

1. Set fine-mesh strainer over heatproof bowl. Heat oil and shallots in medium saucepan over medium-high heat, stirring frequently, until shallots are deep golden brown, 10 to 14 minutes. Using slotted spoon, transfer shallots to second bowl. Add garlic to hot oil in saucepan and cook, stirring constantly, until golden brown, 2 to 3 minutes. Using slotted spoon, transfer garlic to bowl with shallots. Add arbols and half of reserved seeds to hot oil and cook, stirring constantly, until arbols turn deep red, 1 to 2 minutes. Strain oil through prepared strainer into bowl; reserve oil and transfer arbols to bowl with shallots and garlic. Do not wash saucepan.

PEANUT-SESAME SAUCE

Makes ⅔ cup

Chunky peanut butter helps this Asian-inspired sauce turn spectacularly rich and creamy once processed. We love the way the thick sauce clings to ingredients in noodle bowls, as in our Peanut Soba Noodle Bowl (page 129).

3	tablespoons chunky peanut butter
3	tablespoons toasted sesame seeds
2	tablespoons soy sauce
1½	tablespoons rice vinegar
1½	tablespoons packed light brown sugar
1½	teaspoons grated fresh ginger
1	garlic clove, minced
¾	teaspoon hot sauce

Process all ingredients in blender until smooth and mixture has consistency of heavy cream, about 1 minute (adjust consistency with warm water, 1 table-spoon at a time, as needed). Season with salt and pepper to taste. (Sauce can be refrigerated for up to 3 days; add warm water as needed to loosen before using.)

TAHINI SAUCE

Makes 1¼ cups

Nutty tahini and tart lemon juice combine to form a creamy sauce with Middle Eastern flair. The flavorful sauce can be used as a thick dressing, as in our Fattoush Salad Bowl (page 45).

½	cup tahini
½	cup water
¼	cup lemon juice (2 lemons)
2	garlic cloves, minced

Whisk all ingredients together in bowl. Let sit until flavors meld, about 30 minutes. Season with salt and pepper to taste. (Sauce can be refrigerated for up to 4 days.)

HARISSA

Makes ½ cup

Harissa is a traditional North African condiment that is great for flavoring soups, sauces, and dressings. If you can't find Aleppo pepper, you can substitute ¾ teaspoon paprika and ¾ teaspoon finely chopped red pepper flakes.

6	tablespoons extra-virgin olive oil
6	garlic cloves, minced
2	tablespoons paprika
1	tablespoon ground coriander
1	tablespoon ground dried Aleppo pepper
1	teaspoon ground cumin
¾	teaspoon caraway seeds
½	teaspoon table salt

Combine all ingredients in bowl and microwave until bubbling and very fragrant, about 1 minute, stirring halfway through microwaving; let cool to room temperature. (Harissa can be refrigerated for up to 4 days.)

ZHOUG
Makes ½ cup

Zhoug is an Israeli hot sauce that can be either red or green; it adds instant spice to grain bowls, noodle bowls, and even soup bowls. Our vibrant green version is made with fresh herbs, chiles, and spices.

- 6 tablespoons extra-virgin olive oil
- ½ teaspoon ground coriander
- ¼ teaspoon ground cumin
- ¼ teaspoon ground cardamom
- ¼ teaspoon table salt
- Pinch ground cloves
- ¾ cup fresh cilantro leaves
- ½ cup fresh parsley leaves
- 2 green Thai chiles, stemmed and chopped
- 2 garlic cloves, minced

1. Microwave oil, coriander, cumin, cardamom, salt, and cloves in covered bowl until fragrant, about 30 seconds; let cool to room temperature.

2. Pulse oil-spice mixture, cilantro, parsley, chiles, and garlic in food processor until coarse paste forms, about 15 pulses, scraping down sides of bowl as needed. (Zhoug can be refrigerated for up to 4 days.)

CHIMICHURRI SAUCE
Makes ½ cup

This bright, herby Argentinian sauce comes together quickly with the help of a food processor.

- 1 cup fresh parsley leaves
- ¼ cup extra-virgin olive oil
- 1 tablespoon red wine vinegar
- 2 garlic cloves, minced
- ½ teaspoon dried oregano
- ¼ teaspoon red pepper flakes

Pulse all ingredients in food processor until coarsely chopped, about 10 pulses, scraping down sides of bowl as needed. Season with salt and pepper to taste. (Sauce can be refrigerated for up to 3 days.)

RANCH DRESSING
Makes 1½ cups

Ranch dressing is a classic for salads, but most store-bought versions have lackluster flavor. For intense herb flavor and creaminess, we love our simply whisked homemade version.

- ⅔ cup plain yogurt
- ½ cup buttermilk
- ¼ cup sour cream
- 1 tablespoon minced shallot or red onion
- 1 tablespoon minced fresh parsley
- 1 tablespoon minced fresh dill
- 1 garlic clove, minced
- 1 teaspoon lemon juice
- ½ teaspoon table salt
- ¼ teaspoon coarsely ground pepper
- Pinch sugar

Whisk all ingredients together in bowl. Season with salt and pepper to taste. (Dressing can be refrigerated for up to 4 days; whisk to recombine before using.)

BLUE CHEESE DRESSING
Makes 1½ cups

Blue cheese dressing adds tangy, creamy, funky flavor to just about any salad bowl. This recipe can be easily doubled.

- 1 cup plain yogurt
- 2 ounces blue cheese, crumbled (½ cup)
- 2 tablespoons plus 2 teaspoons lemon juice
- 2 garlic cloves, minced
- ½ teaspoon table salt

Whisk all ingredients together in bowl. Season with salt and pepper to taste. (Dressing can be refrigerated for up to 4 days; whisk to recombine before using.)

GREEN GODDESS DRESSING

Makes 1¼ cups

An abundance of herbs gives this boldly flavored dressing its name along with its green color.

 1 tablespoon lemon juice
 1 tablespoon water
 2 teaspoons dried tarragon
 ½ cup buttermilk
 ¼ cup plain yogurt
 ¼ cup sour cream
 ¼ cup minced fresh parsley
 1 garlic clove, minced
 1 anchovy fillet, minced (optional)
 ¼ cup minced fresh chives
 ¼ teaspoon table salt
 ¼ teaspoon pepper

1. Combine lemon juice, water, and tarragon in small bowl and let sit for 15 minutes.

2. Process tarragon mixture, buttermilk, yogurt, sour cream, parsley, garlic, and anchovy, if using, in blender until smooth, scraping down sides of blender jar as needed; transfer dressing to clean bowl. Stir in chives, salt, and pepper. Cover and refrigerate until flavors meld, about 1 hour. Season with salt and pepper to taste. (Dressing can be refrigerated for up to 4 days; whisk to recombine before using.)

CREAMY AVOCADO DRESSING

Makes 1 cup

Rich avocado makes for a deliciously creamy dressing with no dairy needed.

 1 ripe avocado, halved, pitted, and cut into
   ½-inch pieces
 2 tablespoons extra-virgin olive oil
 1 teaspoon grated lemon zest, plus
   3 tablespoons juice
 1 garlic clove, minced
 ¾ teaspoon table salt
 ¼ teaspoon pepper

Process all ingredients in food processor until smooth, about 30 seconds, scraping down sides of bowl as needed. Season with salt and pepper to taste. (Dressing can be refrigerated for up to 5 days; whisk to recombine before using.)

CREAMY ROASTED GARLIC DRESSING

Makes 1 cup

This dairy-free dressing gets its hearty texture and body from garlic. Three whole heads are roasted for a mellow sweet-savory flavor that you'll want to add to everything.

 3 large garlic heads (3 ounces each), outer
   papery skins removed and top third of heads
   cut off and discarded
 ¼ cup white wine vinegar
 3 tablespoons water
 2 teaspoons honey
 1 teaspoon Dijon mustard
 1 teaspoon minced fresh thyme
 ¼ teaspoon table salt
 ¼ teaspoon pepper
 ⅓ cup extra-virgin olive oil

1. Adjust oven rack to middle position and heat oven to 350 degrees. Wrap garlic in aluminum foil and roast until golden brown and very tender, 1 to 1¼ hours. Remove garlic from oven and carefully open foil packet. When garlic is cool enough to handle, squeeze cloves from skins (you should have about 6 tablespoons); discard skins.

2. Process garlic, vinegar, water, honey, mustard, thyme, salt, and pepper in blender until smooth, about 45 seconds, scraping down sides of blender jar as needed. With blender running, slowly add oil until combined, about 1 minute. Season with salt and pepper to taste. (Dressing can be refrigerated for up to 1 week; whisk to recombine before serving.)

CREAMLESS CREAMY DRESSING

Makes 2 cups

For an all-purpose dairy-free creamy dressing, we turned to cashews to achieve the perfect consistency. You'll need a conventional blender for this recipe; an immersion blender or food processor will produce dressing that is grainy and thin. Use raw unsalted cashews, not roasted, to ensure the proper flavor balance.

    1 cup raw cashews
    ¾ cup water, plus extra as needed
    3 tablespoons cider vinegar
  1¼ teaspoons table salt
    1 teaspoon onion powder
    ½ teaspoon sugar
    ¼ teaspoon garlic powder
    2 tablespoons minced fresh chives
    1 tablespoon minced fresh parsley
    ½ teaspoon pepper

1. Process cashews in blender on low speed to consistency of fine gravel mixed with sand, 10 to 15 seconds. Add water, vinegar, salt, onion powder, sugar, and garlic powder and process on low speed until combined, about 5 seconds. Let mixture sit for 15 minutes.

2. Process on low speed until all ingredients are well blended, about 1 minute. Scrape down blender jar. Process on high speed until dressing is smooth and creamy, 3 to 4 minutes. Transfer dressing to bowl. Cover and refrigerate until cold, about 45 minutes. Stir in chives, parsley, and pepper. Thin with extra water, adding 1 tablespoon at a time, to desired consistency. Season with salt and pepper to taste. (Dressing can be refrigerated for up to 1 week.)

VARIATIONS
Creamless Creamy Ginger-Miso Dressing

Omit salt, garlic powder, chives, and parsley. Decrease water to ⅔ cup. Substitute ¼ cup rice vinegar for cider vinegar, 2 tablespoons white miso for onion powder, 2 tablespoons soy sauce for sugar, and 2 tablespoons grated fresh ginger for pepper. Add 1 teaspoon toasted sesame oil with water in step 1.

Creamless Creamy Green Goddess Dressing

Omit onion powder. Decrease cashews to ¾ cup, salt to ¾ teaspoon, and pepper to ¼ teaspoon. Substitute lemon juice for cider vinegar and 2 rinsed anchovy fillets for sugar (or omit for a vegan dressing). Increase parsley to ⅓ cup and chives to ⅓ cup. Add 1 tablespoon chopped fresh tarragon to water mixture in step 1.

Creamless Creamy Roasted Red Pepper and Tahini Dressing

Decrease cashews to ½ cup and increase garlic powder to ½ teaspoon. Substitute 1 (12-ounce) jar roasted red peppers, drained and chopped coarse, for water. Substitute sherry vinegar for cider vinegar and 3 tablespoons tahini for onion powder. Substitute 2 teaspoons toasted sesame oil for sugar and ½ teaspoon smoked paprika for pepper. Increase salt to 1½ teaspoons and add pinch cayenne pepper to bell pepper mixture in step 1. Omit chives and parsley.

TZATZIKI

Makes 2 cups

This Mediterranean yogurt sauce adds cool, herby flavor to any bowl. Using Greek yogurt here is key; do not substitute regular plain yogurt or the sauce will be very watery.

- 1 (12-ounce) cucumber, peeled, halved lengthwise, seeded, and shredded
- ½ teaspoon table salt
- 1 cup whole-milk Greek yogurt
- 2 tablespoons extra-virgin olive oil
- 2 tablespoons minced fresh mint and/or dill
- 1 small garlic clove, minced

1. Toss cucumber with salt in colander and let drain for 15 minutes.

2. Whisk yogurt, oil, mint, and garlic together in bowl, then stir in drained cucumber. Cover and refrigerate until chilled, at least 1 hour. Season with salt and pepper to taste. (Tzatziki can be refrigerated for up to 2 days.)

VARIATION
Beet Tzatziki

Reduce amount of cucumber to 6 ounces and add 6 ounces raw beets, peeled and grated, to cucumber and salt in step 1.

YOGURT SAUCE

Makes 1 cup

Creamy yogurt makes for a simple sauce perfect to drizzle over a variety of green or grain bowls. Do not substitute low-fat or nonfat yogurt here.

- 1 cup plain whole-milk yogurt
- 1 teaspoon grated lemon zest plus 2 tablespoons juice
- 1 garlic clove, minced

Whisk all ingredients together in bowl. Cover and refrigerate until flavors meld, at least 30 minutes. Season with salt and pepper to taste. (Sauce can be refrigerated for up to 4 days.)

VARIATIONS
Tahini-Yogurt Sauce

Add ⅓ cup tahini.

Herb-Yogurt Sauce

Add 2 tablespoons minced fresh cilantro and 2 tablespoons minced fresh mint.

Chipotle-Yogurt Sauce

Substitute lime zest and juice for lemon zest and juice. Add 1 tablespoon minced canned chipotle in adobo sauce.

· ·

SPICY AVOCADO–SOUR CREAM SAUCE

Makes 1 cup

For a spicy, rich sauce that can stand up to hefty toppings, we combined avocado and sour cream.

- 1 cup sour cream
- ½ ripe avocado, cut into 1-inch pieces
- 1 jalapeño chile, stemmed, seeded, and chopped
- 1 teaspoon lime juice

Process all ingredients in food processor until smooth, scraping down sides of bowl as needed. Season with salt and pepper to taste. (Sauce can be refrigerated for up to 2 days.)

Orange-Avocado Relish

Substitute 1 large orange for grapefruits; quarter orange before slicing crosswise. Substitute 2 tablespoons minced fresh cilantro for basil, and 4 teaspoons lime juice for lemon juice. Add 1 diced avocado and 1 small minced jalapeño chile to juice mixture with orange.

....

ONE-MINUTE TOMATO SALSA

Makes 3 cups

For bright, fresh salsa that requires about as much effort as opening a jar, we turned to the food processor to give us delicious flavor in record time.

- ½ small red onion, cut into 1-inch pieces
- ½ cup fresh cilantro leaves
- ¼ cup jarred sliced jalapeños
- 2 tablespoons lime juice
- 2 garlic cloves, chopped
- ½ teaspoon table salt
- 1 (28-ounce) can diced tomatoes, drained

Pulse onion, cilantro, jalapeños, lime juice, garlic, and salt in food processor until coarsely chopped, about 5 pulses, scraping down sides of bowl as needed. Add tomatoes and pulse until combined, about 3 pulses. Drain salsa briefly in fine-mesh strainer, then transfer to bowl and season with salt and pepper to taste. (Salsa can be refrigerated for up to 2 days.)

VARIATIONS
One-Minute Tomato and Black Bean Salsa

Add ½ teaspoon chili powder to food processor with onion. Stir 1 cup canned black beans, rinsed, into drained salsa before seasoning.

One-Minute Smoky Tomato and Green Pepper Salsa

Add 1 green bell pepper, stemmed, seeded, and cut into 1-inch pieces, and 1 tablespoon minced canned chipotle chile in adobo sauce to food processor with onion.

GRAPEFRUIT-BASIL RELISH

Makes 1 cup

With a combination of citrus and herbs, this relish boasts bright, fresh-tart flavor. It is especially good with seafood, as in our Shrimp and Grapefruit Salad Bowl (page 43).

- 2 red grapefruits
- 1 small shallot, minced
- 2 tablespoons chopped fresh basil
- 2 teaspoons lemon juice
- 2 teaspoons extra-virgin olive oil or vegetable oil

Cut away peel and pith from grapefruits. Cut grapefruits into 8 wedges, then slice crosswise into ½-inch-thick pieces. Place grapefruits in strainer set over bowl and let drain for 15 minutes; measure out and reserve 1 tablespoon drained juice. Combine reserved juice, shallot, basil, lemon juice, and oil in bowl. Stir in grapefruits and let sit for 15 minutes. Season with salt and pepper to taste. (Relish can be refrigerated for up to 2 days.)

VARIATIONS
Tangerine-Ginger Relish

Substitute 4 tangerines for grapefruits; quarter tangerines before slicing crosswise. Substitute 1½ teaspoons grated fresh ginger for shallot, and 1 thinly sliced scallion for basil.

nutritional information for our recipes

To calculate the nutritional values of our recipes per serving, we used The Food Processor SQL by ESHA research. When using this program, we entered all the ingredients, using weights for important baking ingredients such as flour for crusts and fruit for pie fillings. We also used our preferred brands in these analyses. Any ingredient listed as "optional" was excluded from the analyses. If there is a range in the serving size, we used the highest number of servings to calculate the nutritional values.

BOWLS

	CALORIES	TOTAL FAT (G)	SAT FAT (G)	CHOL (MG)	SODIUM (MG)	TOTAL CARB (G)	DIETARY FIBER (G)	TOTAL SUGARS (G)	PROTEIN (G)
Salad Bowls									
Green Goodness Salad Bowl	480	24	4.5	135	810	17	7	5	49
Sriracha-Lime Tofu Salad Bowl	280	16	1.5	0	410	20	5	11	13
Harvest Bowl	400	24	6	25	790	40	6	20	7
California Chicken Salad Bowl	430	19	3	125	1010	21	7	11	43
Quinoa Taco Salad Bowl	360	17	3.5	10	400	44	12	7	13
Buffalo Chicken Bowl	380	13	6	150	1460	16	4	9	47
Thai Steak Salad Bowl	390	26	5	75	750	11	3	4	27
Seared Tuna Poke Bowl	430	25	3.5	45	810	19	4	5	30
Mediterranean Tuna Salad Bowl	390	25	3.5	30	900	18	5	3	23
Moroccan Chicken Salad Bowl	550	29	4.5	125	1000	27	4	14	44
Steakhouse Salad Bowl	400	21	7	85	790	22	4	16	32
Mediterranean Chopped Salad Bowl	310	20	4	15	1070	26	7	5	9
Smoked Salmon Niçoise Bowl	320	15	5	220	960	25	4	5	21
Shrimp and Grapefruit Salad Bowl	470	25	3.5	215	1010	32	12	11	29
Fattoush Salad Bowl	320	21	3	0	420	27	8	3	11
Winter Salad Bowl	410	18	3.5	85	970	40	8	18	27
Kale Cobb Salad Bowl	450	28	8	205	700	14	6	5	39
Steak Fajita Salad Bowl	420	22	6	85	700	28	5	10	31
Rainbow Bowl	560	29	3.5	0	460	58	10	25	21
Meze Salad Bowl	410	26	10	30	690	34	5	23	13
Bistro Salad Bowl	410	29	8	215	900	19	2	2	15
Grain & Bean Bowls									
Skillet Burrito Bowl	760	30	10	105	1000	86	7	6	38
Weeknight Bibimbap	580	24	3.5	185	1470	74	3	11	19
Green Fried Rice Bowl	570	26	3	185	930	67	5	4	17
Sichuan Stir-Fry Bowl	540	20	5	40	1040	80	12	10	20

	CALORIES	TOTAL FAT (G)	SAT FAT (G)	CHOL (MG)	SODIUM (MG)	TOTAL CARB (G)	DIETARY FIBER (G)	TOTAL SUGARS (G)	PROTEIN (G)
Grain & Bean Bowls (continued)									
Tofu Sushi Bowl	530	22	2	0	840	73	9	3	17
Forbidden Rice Bowl with Salmon	690	30	7	100	570	61	7	7	42
Buddha Bowl	550	33	4.5	0	1010	56	20	12	14
Italian Harvest Bowl	720	32	6	10	910	102	8	26	16
Farro Bowl with Tofu, Mushrooms, and Spinach	680	33	3	5	790	78	2	9	22
Chimichurri Couscous Bowl	710	31	4	0	520	83	3	4	26
Smoked Trout and Couscous Bowl	650	25	8	50	510	74	0	4	27
Thanksgiving Quinoa Bowl	600	24	4	85	830	65	7	13	33
Pork Mojo Quinoa Bowl	650	24	4	105	770	62	8	14	45
Egyptian Barley Bowl	580	29	6	15	670	73	11	22	9
Turkey Meatball and Barley Bowl	620	23	7	50	560	67	10	10	38
Golden Bulgur Bowl	650	30	8	95	1230	66	12	20	34
Bulgur, Pork, and Pesto Bowl	680	32	6	105	1120	57	11	12	44
Shredded Pork and Pinto Bean Tostada Bowl	680	28	4.5	105	1460	62	18	9	49
Shakshuka Bowl	470	23	6	200	1400	48	12	18	22
Pantry Chickpea Bowl	390	22	4.5	190	740	31	11	2	20
Polenta Bowl with Broccoli Rabe and Fried Eggs	420	26	8	210	990	30	6	4	19
Shrimp and Grits Bowl	720	38	19	295	1140	54	3	7	40
Noodle Bowls									
Chicken Chow Mein Bowl	550	18	2	125	1470	59	1	8	38
Singapore Noodle Bowl	450	15	1	150	860	58	3	8	21
Pork Lo Mein Bowl	650	24	3	150	1320	60	3	8	47
Summer Ramen Bowl	530	13	1.5	95	1160	72	4	6	32
Yaki Udon Bowl	520	22	9	90	1510	63	6	12	37
Saucy Udon Noodle Bowl	350	12	1.5	0	1110	60	5	16	15
Bun Cha Noodle Bowl	600	28	9	80	950	62	1	10	25
Shrimp Pad Thai Bowl	590	25	2.5	200	1100	72	1	19	21
Spicy Basil Noodle Bowl	530	18	1	0	850	76	4	20	17
Creamy Miso-Ginger Noodle Bowl	500	25	3	5	910	60	1	9	11
Pork and Eggplant Soba Noodle Bowl with Miso	640	31	10	65	1280	68	4	9	24
Peanut Soba Noodle Bowl	660	18	3	125	1670	67	2	9	57
Indian-Spiced Chicken Zoodle Bowl	350	15	3	90	390	23	3	18	31
Shrimp Saganaki Zoodle Bowl	340	23	4.5	120	920	18	3	8	19
Mediterranean Carrot Noodle Bowl	350	18	6	15	560	43	9	28	9
Lemony Linguine Bowl	530	22	3.5	5	460	69	1	2	15

	CALORIES	TOTAL FAT (G)	SAT FAT (G)	CHOL (MG)	SODIUM (MG)	TOTAL CARB (G)	DIETARY FIBER (G)	TOTAL SUGARS (G)	PROTEIN (G)
Noodle Bowls (continued)									
Spinach Pesto Noodle Bowl	500	13	2.5	5	1060	79	4	9	18
Creamy Corn Bucatini Bowl	590	11	4.5	25	540	101	2	10	24
Roasted Cauliflower and Brown Butter Noodle Bowl	690	38	16	60	710	75	5	6	16
Tagliatelle alla Norma Bowl	550	19	4	15	1190	80	5	12	16
Soup Bowls									
Curried Coconut Shrimp Soup	510	29	17	215	1530	31	4	9	32
Vietnamese Beef Pho	520	7	2	60	1170	75	1	5	37
Mexican Street-Corn Chowder	420	23	4.5	25	930	46	7	14	20
Green Pork Posole Bowl	550	30	10	85	1150	40	10	15	31
Gazpacho Bowl	80	0	0	0	1030	16	3	10	3
Turkey Chili Bowl	450	16	5	60	1260	40	11	4	42
Caldo Verde Bowl	370	22	7	35	1160	25	2	1	16
Creamy Butternut Squash Soup with Apples and Pork	390	18	8	55	850	45	8	14	17
Mediterranean Eggplant Soup with Lamb	350	22	7	40	1070	25	7	13	18
Chicken Tortilla Soup with Chard	320	10	1	85	1170	26	1	6	31
Black Bean Soup	300	13	1.5	0	1230	39	14	5	14
Thai-Style Hot and Sour Soup	220	1.5	0	105	910	32	1	5	19
Hearty Cabbage Soup	420	19	8	60	920	34	6	10	24
Quinoa and Vegetable Stew	350	13	2.5	10	640	46	6	7	14
Kimchi Beef-Noodle Soup	590	12	3	60	1220	83	0	14	26
North African Vegetable and Bean Stew	350	20	3.5	5	1150	32	6	7	13
Ramen Zoodle Bowl	310	22	2.5	0	1280	19	3	11	12
Acquacotta Bowl	490	23	3	0	1390	54	13	13	16
Vegetable Shabu-Shabu Bowl	360	5	0	0	1300	52	3	20	18
Bowl Basics									
GRAINS & NOODLES									
Simple White Rice Pilaf	300	7	1	0	300	54	0	0	6
Big Batch Simple White Rice Pilaf	200	2	0	0	340	41	0	0	5
Hands-Off Baked Brown Rice	270	8	0.5	0	300	53	5	0	5
Big Batch Hands-Off Baked Brown Rice	250	5	0	0	290	53	5	0	5
Quinoa Pilaf	230	4	0	0	300	41	4	2	9
Big Batch Quinoa Pilaf	230	4	0	0	300	41	4	2	9
Creamy Parmesan Polenta	200	10	6	25	590	20	2	0	8
Big Batch Creamy Parmesan Polenta	160	7	3.5	15	770	20	2	0	6

	CALORIES	TOTAL FAT (G)	SAT FAT (G)	CHOL (MG)	SODIUM (MG)	TOTAL CARB (G)	DIETARY FIBER (G)	TOTAL SUGARS (G)	PROTEIN (G)
Bowl Basics (continued)									
PROTEINS									
Perfect Poached Chicken	210	4.5	1	125	520	0	0	0	39
Seared Chicken Breasts	230	7	1.5	125	370	0	0	0	38
Roast Pork Tenderloin	200	6	1.5	105	380	0	0	0	34
Pan-Seared Flank Steak	210	12	4	75	350	0	0	0	24
Sautéed Shrimp	180	9	1	215	540	2	0	0	23
Chipotle Shrimp	180	9	1	215	540	2	0	0	23
Lemony Shrimp	180	9	1	215	540	2	0	0	23
Oven-Roasted Salmon	380	25	5	95	390	0	0	0	35
Juniper and Fennel Roasted Salmon	390	25	5	95	390	2	0	1	35
Crispy Tempeh	60	3	0	0	80	4	0	2	5
Pan-Seared Tofu	300	18	1.5	0	190	20	0	0	15
Gingery Stir-Fried Edamame	100	6	0	0	150	1	0	0	8
Easy-Peel Hard-Cooked Eggs	70	5	1.5	185	70	0	0	0	6
Easy-Peel Soft-Cooked Eggs	70	5	1.5	185	70	0	0	0	6
Fried Eggs	90	7	1.5	185	220	0	0	0	6
SPICE RUBS									
Cajun-Style Rub (1 tbsp)	10	0	0	0	1620	2	1	0	0
Barbecue Rub (1 tbsp)	30	0	0	0	90	7	1	5	1
Herbes de Provence (1 tbsp)	10	0	0	0	0	2	1	0	0
Five-Spice Powder (1 tbsp)	10	0	0	0	0	3	2	0	0
VEGETABLES									
Pan-Roasted Asparagus	25	1	0	0	0	2	1	1	1
Roasted Beets	50	0	0	0	90	11	3	8	2
Sautéed Broccoli with Garlic and Thyme	60	5	1	0	90	3	1	1	2
with Sesame Oil and Ginger	60	5	0	0	90	3	1	1	2
Roasted Butternut Squash	120	3.5	0.5	0	300	22	4	4	2
Roasted Carrots	130	7	1	0	410	16	5	8	2
Sautéed Cherry Tomatoes	30	1.5	0	0	0	5	1	3	1
Roasted Cauliflower	90	7	1	0	180	6	2	2	2
Spicy Roasted Cauliflower	90	7	1	0	200	6	3	2	2
Marinated Eggplant with Capers and Mint	90	7	1	0	160	5	2	3	1
Simple Sautéed Green Beans with Garlic	25	0.5	0	0	40	4	2	2	1
Sautéed Mushrooms with Shallots and Thyme	45	2	1	5	160	4	0	3	1
with Sesame and Ginger	60	3.5	0	0	280	4	0	3	2

	CALORIES	TOTAL FAT (G)	SAT FAT (G)	CHOL (MG)	SODIUM (MG)	TOTAL CARB (G)	DIETARY FIBER (G)	TOTAL SUGARS (G)	PROTEIN (G)
Bowl Basics (continued)									
Roasted Bell Peppers	30	0	0	0	0	5	2	4	1
Sautéed Radishes	40	3	2	10	105	3	1	2	1
with Chili	40	3	2	10	110	3	2	2	1
with Vadouvan Curry and Almonds	70	5	2	10	105	4	2	2	2
Snap Peas with Lemon, Garlic, and Basil	35	1.5	0	0	75	4	1	2	2
Sesame Snap Peas	45	2	0	0	190	5	1	3	2
Spaghetti Squash with Basil and Parmesan	80	5	1	5	150	7	2	3	2
with Asian Flavors	70	4	0.5	0	210	7	2	3	1
Roasted Sweet Potatoes	120	3.5	0	0	210	20	3	6	2
TOPPINGS									
Quick Toasted Nuts (2 tbsp)	110	10	1	0	150	4	2	1	4
Rosemary Nuts (2 tbsp)	110	10	1	0	150	4	2	1	4
Orange-Fennel Nuts (2 tbsp)	110	10	1	0	150	4	2	1	4
Spiced Nuts (2 tbsp)	110	10	1	0	150	4	2	1	4
Lemon-Garlic Nuts (2 tbsp)	110	10	1	0	150	4	2	1	4
Spiced Pepitas or Sunflower Seeds (1 tbsp)	60	5	1	0	75	1	1	0	2
Savory Seed Brittle (2 tbsp)	80	5	1	0	135	6	1	2	3
Pistachio Dukkah (1 tbsp)	30	2.5	0	0	120	2	1	0	1
Crispy Chickpeas (2 tbsp)	70	4	0.5	0	140	6	2	0	2
Indian-Spiced Crispy Chickpeas (2 tbsp)	70	4	0.5	0	140	6	2	0	2
Barbecue-Spiced Crispy Chickpeas (2 tbsp)	70	4	0.5	0	140	7	2	0	2
Spanish-Spiced Crispy Chickpeas (2 tbsp)	70	4	0.5	0	140	6	2	0	2
Crispy Shallots (1 tbsp)	15	1	0	0	0	1	0	0	0
Garlic Chips (1 tbsp)	20	2	0	0	0	1	0	0	0
Pita Crumble (¼ cup)	40	2.5	0	0	75	4	0	0	1
Frico Crumble (2 tbsp)	35	2.5	1.5	10	115	0	0	0	2
Vegan Parmesan Substitute (2 tbsp)	60	5	1	0	160	3	0	1	3
Crispy Tortilla Strips (¼ cup)	80	3	0	0	10	14	0	2	2
Croutons (2 tbsp)	60	4	2	10	25	4	0	1	1
Garlic Croutons (2 tbsp)	60	4	2	10	25	4	0	1	1
Buttery Rye Croutons (2 tbsp)	50	4	2	10	35	3	0	0	0
Crispy Rice Noodles (½ cup)	30	2	0	0	0	3	0	0	0
QUICK PICKLES									
Quick Pickled Grapes (2 tbsp)	15	0	0	0	30	4	0	4	0
Quick Pickled Fennel (¼ cup)	10	0	0	0	15	2	1	1	0
Quick Sweet and Spicy Pickled Red Onions (2 tbsp)	25	0	0	0	50	5	0	5	0
Quick Pickled Carrot Ribbons (¼ cup)	25	0	0	0	80	5	1	3	0

	CALORIES	TOTAL FAT (G)	SAT FAT (G)	CHOL (MG)	SODIUM (MG)	TOTAL CARB (G)	DIETARY FIBER (G)	TOTAL SUGARS (G)	PROTEIN (G)
Bowl Basics (continued)									
DRESSINGS & SAUCES									
Make-Ahead Vinaigrette (2 tbsp)	210	22	2.5	0	200	2	0	2	0
Pomegranate-Honey Vinaigrette (2 tbsp)	80	3.5	0	0	150	11	0	11	0
Apple Cider–Sage Vinaigrette (2 tbsp)	70	3.5	0	0	150	10	0	9	0
Orange-Ginger Vinaigrette (2 tbsp)	70	3.5	0.5	0	150	9	0	7	1
Sriracha-Lime Vinaigrette (2 tbsp)	110	9	1.5	0	210	6	0	5	1
Sesame-Scallion Vinaigrette (2 tbsp)	20	0	0	0	610	2	0	2	1
Sesame Sauce (1 tbsp)	90	7	1	0	170	4	1	2	2
Thai Chili Jam (1 tbsp)	60	4.5	0	0	115	5	0	3	1
Gochujang Sauce (2 tbsp)	110	7	1	0	350	11	0	6	1
Miso-Ginger Sauce (2 tbsp)	100	9	1.5	5	430	4	0	3	1
Peanut-Sesame Sauce (2 tbsp)	110	7	1.5	0	400	8	1	5	4
Tahini Sauce (2 tbsp)	70	6	1	0	0	3	1	0	2
Harissa (1 tbsp)	110	11	1.5	0	150	2	1	0	1
Zhoug (1 tbsp)	100	11	1.5	0	75	1	0	0	0
Chimichurri Sauce (2 tbsp)	140	14	2	0	10	2	1	0	1
Ranch Dressing (2 tbsp)	20	1.5	1	5	115	2	0	1	1
Blue Cheese Dressing (2 tbsp)	30	2	1.5	5	170	1	0	1	2
Green Goddess Dressing (2 tbsp)	20	1.5	0.5	5	75	2	0	1	1
Creamy Avocado Dressing (2 tbsp)	70	7	1	0	220	3	2	0	1
Creamy Roasted Garlic Dressing (2 tbsp)	130	9	1.5	0	95	11	1	2	2
Creamless Creamy Dressing (2 tbsp)	50	4	0.5	0	180	3	0	1	2
Ginger-Miso Dressing (2 tbsp)	60	4.5	0.5	0	180	5	0	1	2
Green Goddess Dressing (2 tbsp)	40	3	0.5	0	110	2	0	0	1
Roasted Red Pepper and Tahini Dressing (2 tbsp)	50	4	0.5	0	280	3	0	1	1
Tzatziki (¼ cup)	80	7	3	5	160	2	0	2	3
Beet Tzatziki (¼ cup)	90	7	3	5	170	4	1	3	3
Yogurt Sauce (2 tbsp)	20	1	0.5	5	15	2	0	2	1
Tahini-Yogurt Sauce (2 tbsp)	80	6	1.5	5	20	4	1	2	3
Herb-Yogurt Sauce (2 tbsp)	20	1	0.5	5	15	2	0	2	1
Chipotle-Yogurt Sauce (2 tbsp)	20	1	0.5	5	15	2	0	2	1
Spicy Avocado–Sour Cream Sauce (2 tbsp)	70	6	2.5	15	25	2	1	1	1
Grapefruit-Basil Relish (¼ cup)	80	2.5	0	0	0	17	6	10	1
Tangerine-Ginger Relish (¼ cup)	70	2.5	0	0	0	12	2	9	1
Orange-Avocado Relish (¼ cup)	120	10	1.5	0	35	9	4	4	1
One-Minute Tomato Salsa (½ cup)	30	0	0	0	570	7	0	3	1
One-Minute Tomato and Black Bean Salsa (½ cup)	60	0	0	0	590	13	4	3	3
One-Minute Smoky Tomato and Green Pepper Salsa (½ cup)	50	0	0	0	640	10	3	4	2

conversions & equivalents

Some say cooking is a science and an art. We would say geography has a hand in it, too. Flours and sugars manufactured in the United Kingdom and elsewhere will feel and taste different from those manufactured in the United States. So we cannot promise that a loaf of bread you bake in Canada or England will taste the same as a loaf baked in the States, but we can offer guidelines for converting weights and measures. We also recommend that you rely on your instincts when making our recipes. Refer to the visual cues provided. If the dough hasn't come together as described, you may need to add more flour—even if the recipe doesn't tell you to. You be the judge.

The recipes in this book were developed using standard U.S. measures following U.S. government guidelines. The charts below offer equivalents for U.S. and metric measures. All conversions are approximate and have been rounded up or down to the nearest whole number.

example
   1 teaspoon = 4.9292 milliliters, rounded up to 5 milliliters
   1 ounce = 28.3495 grams, rounded down to 28 grams

VOLUME CONVERSIONS

U.S.	METRIC
1 teaspoon	5 milliliters
2 teaspoons	10 milliliters
1 tablespoon	15 milliliters
2 tablespoons	30 milliliters
¼ cup	59 milliliters
⅓ cup	79 milliliters
½ cup	118 milliliters
¾ cup	177 milliliters
1 cup	237 milliliters
1¼ cups	296 milliliters
1½ cups	355 milliliters
2 cups (1 pint)	473 milliliters
2½ cups	591 milliliters
3 cups	710 milliliters
4 cups (1 quart)	0.946 liter
1.06 quarts	1 liter
4 quarts (1 gallon)	3.8 liters

WEIGHT CONVERSIONS

OUNCES	GRAMS
½	14
¾	21
1	28
1½	43
2	57
2½	71
3	85
3½	99
4	113
4½	128
5	142
6	170
7	198
8	227
9	255
10	283
12	340
16 (1 pound)	454

CONVERSIONS FOR COMMON BAKING INGREDIENTS

Because measuring by weight is far more accurate than measuring by volume, and thus more likely to produce reliable results, in our recipes we provide ounce measures in addition to cup measures for many ingredients. Refer to the chart below to convert these measures into grams.

INGREDIENT	OUNCES	GRAMS
Flour		
1 cup all-purpose flour*	5	142
1 cup cake flour	4	113
1 cup whole-wheat flour	5½	156
Sugar		
1 cup granulated (white) sugar	7	198
1 cup packed brown sugar (light or dark)	7	198
1 cup confectioners' sugar	4	113
Cocoa Powder		
1 cup cocoa powder	3	85
Butter†		
4 tablespoons (½ stick or ¼ cup)	2	57
8 tablespoons (1 stick or ½ cup)	4	113
16 tablespoons (2 sticks or 1 cup)	8	227

* U.S. all-purpose flour, the most frequently used flour in this book, does not contain leaveners, as some European flours do. These leavened flours are called self-rising or self-raising. If you are using self-rising flour, take this into consideration before adding leaveners to a recipe.

† In the United States, butter is sold both salted and unsalted. We recommend unsalted butter. If you are using salted butter, take this into consideration before adding salt to a recipe.

OVEN TEMPERATURE

FAHRENHEIT	CELSIUS	GAS MARK
225	105	¼
250	120	½
275	135	1
300	150	2
325	165	3
350	180	4
375	190	5
400	200	6
425	220	7
450	230	8
475	245	9

CONVERTING TEMPERATURES FROM AN INSTANT-READ THERMOMETER

We include doneness temperatures in many of the recipes in this book. We recommend an instant-read thermometer for the job. Refer to the table above to convert Fahrenheit degrees to Celsius. Or, for temperatures not represented in the chart, use this simple formula:

Subtract 32 degrees from the Fahrenheit reading, then divide the result by 1.8 to find the Celsius reading.

example
"Flip chicken, brush with remaining glaze, and cook until breast registers 160 degrees, 1 to 3 minutes."

to convert
160°F − 32 = 128°
128° ÷ 1.8 = 71.11°C, rounded down to 71°C

index

Note: Page references in *italics* indicate photographs.

BOWLS